1 0 0 0
YEARS
PEACE

By Wim Malgo

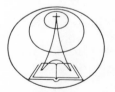

Published by
The Midnight Call Inc.
Hamilton, Ohio

1000
YEARS
PEACE

By Wim Malgo

Copyright 1974 by
The Midnight Call, Inc.
Hamilton, Ohio

Printed in the United States of America
by Hamilton Printing Co., Hamilton, Ohio

Contents

CHAPTER 1

THE REALITY OF THE MILLENNIUM

"And I saw an angel come down from heaven, having the key of the bottomless pit and a great chain in his hand. And he laid hold on the dragon, that old serpent, which is the Devil, and Satan, and bound him a thousand years, and cast him into the bottomless pit, and shut him up, and set a seal upon him, that he should deceive the nations no more, till the thousand years should be fulfilled: and after that he must be loosed a little season. And I saw thrones, and they sat upon them, and judgment was given unto them: and I saw the souls of them that were beheaded for the witness of Jesus, and for the word of God, and which had not worshipped the beast, neither his image, neither had received his mark upon their foreheads, or in their hands; and they lived and reigned with Christ a thousand years. But the rest of the dead lived not again until the thousand years were finished. This is the first resurrection. Blessed and holy is he that hath part in the first resurrection: on such the second death hath no power, but they shall be priests of God and of Christ, and shall reign with him a thousand years" (Revelation 20:1-6).

In this short passage the millennium is mentioned repeatedly. This 1,000 year reign of peace will begin visibly when Satan is bound. He will then be already weakened by the terrible judgments which will come upon the earth during and after the great tribulation period, for where sin is judged, Satan has nothing more to say or do. This is the secret of Calvary. Jesus was judged in our place and for our sin, and when we become one with Jesus at the cross of Calvary Satan has no more claim to us and no more power over us. In spite of this God still permits the dragon, Satan, to have great power, even though the judgment is being carried out in heaven and on earth. *"And I saw an angel come down from heaven, having the key of the bottomless pit and a great chain in his hand . . ."* Notice that a great chain is needed, for we are dealing with the most powerful prince, the ruler, of darkness himself. At the time of the destruction of the Antichrist Satan will be spiritually bound, thrown into the abyss and locked up for a thousand years. During those thousand years Satan can no longer deceive the nations or the individual, which will result in absolute peace on earth and worldwide blessing.

What actually is the millennium? First of all it is the answer to Jesus' prayer, "Thy kingdom come. Thy will be done in earth as it is in heaven". The thousand year reign of peace is also the seventh or Sabbath millennium. In the 15th century Luther said, "The world will exist for six thousand years: two thousand years without the law, two thousand years under the law, two thousand years under Jesus Christ and after that will come the seventh period of a thousand years." For the eternal God these thousands of years are like days. On the seventh day God rested from all his works. A thousand years are to Him like a day and one day is like a thousand years. We are drawing near the end of the sixth thousand years since creation.

The patriarchs, the prophets, the kings and the priests looked forward to the thousand year reign of peace. When we read the Bible we are amazed how often this coming kingdom is mentioned. In the Old Testament alone we find about fifty prophecies concerning it. It is always mentioned in connection with the King, the Ruler of the kingdom. *"I shall see him, but not now: there shall come a Star out of Jacob, and a Sceptre shall rise out of Israel, and shall smite the corners of Moab, and destroy all the children of Sheth . . . Out of Jacob shall come he that shall have dominion . . ."* (Numbers 24:17 & 19a). The Gentile prophet Balaam saw this. Also Hannah, the mother of Samuel, saw the coming kingdom and sang about it in her prophetic song, which was inspired by the Holy Spirit, *"The adversaries of the Lord shall be broken to pieces; out of heaven shall he thunder upon them: the Lord shall judge the ends of the earth; and he shall give strength unto his king, and exalt the horn of his anointed"* (1 Samuel 2:10). God the Lord will install His King. We find another prophecy concerning the coming kingdom in Psalm 2, but we also read here of the preceding worldwide revolution which we are already experiencing in part, whether it be under the flag of Mao, Breschnev, Castro or any other revolutionary. The human race is being attacked by the spirit of rebellion. *"Why do the heathen rage, and the people imagine a vain thing? The kings of the earth set themselves, and the rulers take counsel together, against the Lord, and against his anointed, saying, Let us break their bands asunder, and cast away their cords from us. He that sitteth in the heavens shall laugh: the Lord shall have them in derision"* (Psalm 2:1-4). For, *"Then shall he speak unto them in his wrath, and vex them in his sore displeasure. Yet have I set my king upon my holy hill of Zion"* (Psalm 2:5-6). This revolt will come to an end at the revelation of the Antichrist, because the Lord will destroy him with the breath of His mouth, and Satan will be bound for a thousand years. This will be the time when God will inaugurate His King, the Prince of Peace.

The Old Testament also testifies to this King, Jesus Christ, and reveals Him to us very clearly. Isaiah tells of His supernatural conception. *"A virgin shall conceive ... "* The birthplace of the King, which is Bethlehem is mentioned in Micah 5:1. The death of the King is described for us in Isaiah 53, also in Psalm 22. This chapter starts with the exclamation of the dying King, *"My God, my God, why hast thou forsaken me?"* Of the Shepherd's execution we read in Psalm 22:16b, *". . . they pierced my hands and my feet."* This Psalm also tells of His future kingdom which He will establish. *"All the ends of the world shall remember and turn unto the Lord: and all the kindreds of the nations shall worship before thee. For the kingdom is the Lord's and he is the governor among the nations"* (Psalm 22:27-28). This last prophecy refers to events which are still in the future. In Psalm 45:6 we read, *"Thy throne, O God, is for ever and ever: the sceptre of thy kingdom is a right sceptre"*. It is remarkable that the writer of the letter to the Hebrews quotes this verse, *"Thy throne, O God, is for ever and ever"* and then speaks of Jesus, *"For unto which of the angels said he at any time, Thou art my son, this day have I begotten thee? And again, I will be to him a Father, and he shall be to me a Son? And again, when he bringeth in the first begotten into the world, he saith, And let all the angels of God worship him. But unto the Son he saith, Thy throne, O God, is for ever and ever: a sceptre of righteousness is the sceptre of thy kingdom"* (Hebrews 1:5-6 & 8). In Psalms 47 and 48 we also find this thousand year reign of peace prophesied but we learn of it especially from the royal prophet Isaiah. For instance, *"And it shall come to pass in the last days, that the mountain of the Lord's house shall be established in the top of the mountains, and shall be exalted above the hills; and all nations shall flow unto it. And many people shall go and say, Come ye, and let us go up to the mountain of the Lord, to the house of the God of Jacob: and he will teach us of his ways, and we will walk in his paths: for out of Zion shall go forth the law, and the word of the Lord from Jerusalem. And he shall judge among the nations, and shall rebuke many people: and they shall beat their swords into plowshares, and their spears into pruninghooks: nation shall not lift up sword against nation, neither shall they learn war any more. O house of Jacob, come ye, and let us walk in the light of the Lord"* (Isaiah 2:2-5). Here the place is named for us where the Kingdom will be set up. The center of worldwide disarmament and world peace will not be Washington, or Moscow, or Rome, or Geneva, or any other place on earth, but the holy mountain in Jerusalem. When Jesus Christ sits on the throne and rules as King, there can be no more wars. Hatred, gossip, divorce and all other squabbles will be banished. What a wonderful situation; even the animal world will be affected, *"And there shall come forth a rod out of the stem of Jesse, and a Branch shall grow out of his roots: and the spirit of the Lord shall rest upon him . . . And righteousness shall be the girdle of his loins, and faithfulness the girdle of his reins. The wolf also shall dwell with the lamb, and the leopard shall lie down with the kid; and the calf and the young lion and the fatling together; and a little child shall lead them. And the cow and the bear shall feed; their young ones shall lie down together: and the lion shall eat straw like the ox. And the sucking child shall play on the hole of the asp, and the weaned child shall put his hand on the cockatrice' den. They shall not hurt nor destroy in all my holy mountain: for the earth shall be full of knowledge of the Lord, as the waters cover the sea. And in that day there shall be a root of Jesse, which shall stand for an ensign of the people; to it shall the Gentiles seek: and his rest shall be glorious."* (Isaiah 11:1-2a & 5-10). This will be a kingdom of incomparable peace. Surely we can already experience something of it now? When the enemy in our hearts is bound all enmity disappears, together with all fear. Then we are ruled by the One of whom it is written, *"He is our peace"*.

"... and the leopard shall die down with the kid ..." (Isaiah 11:6) Postage stamp issued by the Israeli Post Office Department.

Now let us consider the individual stages in which the Kingdom of God is realized. The whole Bible from beginning to end deals with the fact that Jehovah will be King in all eternity and that all things are of Him, through Him and to Him (Romans 11:36). Everything revolves around the Kingdom of God. Through the fall of man it became apparent that man did not want to acknowledge the absolute sovereignty of God, and therewith he rejected his own sovereignty. Thus man, deceived by Satan, lost the sovereignty which

God gave him, for God had made man ruler over all creation. Psalm 8:4 and 6 contain important statements concerning man's position, *"What is man, that thou art mindful of him? and the son of man, that thou visitest him? Thou madest him to have dominion over the works of thy hands; thou hast put all things under his feet"*. That was before man's fall. These verses actually speak prophetically of Jesus as the "last Adam". God told man to rule over His creation, but through his fall Adam was reduced to the position of a slave. This is why Jesus Christ had to come to — as it says in Acts 15:16 — set up the Kingdom again (the tabernacle of David). How could this take place? How was it possible to set up the Kingdom of God again on this earth, which is still in subjection to the devil? It was accomplished by the Lord Jesus who suffered as our substitute and yet remained a King under all circumstances and never sinned. He wore a royal robe of mockery and a crown of mockery, made of thorns, and a sceptre of mockery, a reed, was placed in His hand. He was even given a royal title and it was written over His head on the criminal's cross, *"Jesus, the king of the Jews"*. Jesus had to become the *"last Adam"* so that the *"first Adam"* could be installed again in his royal office. The result is great and wonderful so that we may exclaim, *" . . . and hath made us kings and priests unto God and his Father; to him be glory and dominion for ever and ever. Amen"* (Revelation 1:6). We are kings again, invisible in the flesh as yet, but the moment is coming when we shall be revealed with Jesus — in the millennium. Why? Because we acknowledge Jesus Christ as King. Is this true in your life? Many children of

God think it is important to know Jesus as Saviour, but it is much more important that He is King. It is the tragedy of many children of God that they fall away from the Lord like Israel at the time of Samuel, and they want an earthly king. When Samuel mourned over this the Lord comforted him with the words, " . . . *they have not rejected thee, but they have rejected me, that I should not reign over them"* (1 Samuel 8:7). Later when Jesus came, the true Anointed One, their Messiah, they cried, *"We will not have this man to rule over us — We have no king but Caesar!"* (Luke 19:14). This tragedy of Israel has repeated itself throughout history. The sovereignty of Christ in our hearts is expressed in our longing — worked by the Holy Spirit — for revival, cleansing and sanctification.

The first phase of the re-establishment of the Kingdom of God is called the *"Kingdom of heaven"*. In Matthew 13 and 25 we see that the Lord Jesus spoke of the Kingdom of heaven continually, " . . . *again the Kingdom of heaven is like unto . . . "* In His parables He also shows us how the enemy tries everything possible to destroy this Kingdom of heaven on earth, as for instance by sowing tares. His work becomes more and more intensive because he knows that his end is near (Revelation 12:12b). Jesus Christ, as Man from heaven, has brought us back the Kingdom of heaven. We find this deep meaning in the words of His testimony to Himself, *"And no man hath ascended up to heaven, but he that came down from heaven, even the Son of man which is in heaven"* (John 3:13). The Lord Jesus was always one with His Father. He walked as man on earth but His spirit was with His Father. *"I and the Father are one."*

The second phase we can call the *"Kingdom of Jesus Christ"*. This is the kingdom which we are now awaiting. At the return of Jesus Christ it will be finally and visibly set up. What has been prepared throughout the centuries in the hearts of believers will then become visible. The Lord Jesus said, *"The kingdom of God is within you"*. It is never His ultimate goal, however, that it should remain in our hearts, but that it should one day be revealed, *"When Christ, who is our life, shall appear, then shall ye also appear with him in glory"* (Colossians 3:4). Our redemption from the power of Satan was determined in the heart of God before the foundation of the world. This redemption was made visible in the death and resurrection of His Son. In the same way, His Kingdom will also become visible. We read of the goal of the Kingdom of Jesus Christ, *"For He hath put all things under his feet . . . And when all things shall be subdued unto him, then shall the Son also himself be subject unto him that put all things under him, that God may be all in all"*. So the millennium is the realization of the complete restoration of the Kingdom of God. When Babylon has fallen the great Hallelujah chorus will resound forever, according to Revelation 19 and 20. We learn from the Scriptures that the eternal God Himself is always the goal, and this should also be so in our lives. *"That we should be to the praise of his glory"* (Ephesians 1:6 & 12).

Whenever the question is asked (which originates in unbelief), whether the coming reign of peace is to be understood literally or symbolically I always ask a counter question, Is the nation of Israel as it exists today in the Middle East a reality or just a symbol? The answer is obvious. The nation of Israel is a living reality! The Christian Church has since olden times committed the sin of claiming for herself the biblical promises of blessing meant for Israel, taking them literally. Where, however, the Scriptures speak of the glorious future of Israel she has spiritualized and symbolized everything, with the exception of the threats of judgment which she was only too willing to connect literally with Israel. The annotations of a Bible of the year 1852 show this quite clearly. Isaiah 60:1, where it says, *"Arise, shine; for thy light is come, and the glory of the Lord is risen upon thee"*, is explained in the margin as follows: "Get up, leave thy former affliction; — this is what God says to His Zion, His believing Church." We find another example in Isaiah 62:1, *"For Zion's sake will I not hold my peace, and for Jerusalem's sake I will not rest, until the righteousness thereof go forth as brightness, and the salvation thereof as a lamp that burneth"*. The annotation says: "For the Church's sake, the spiritual Jerusalem, because I love her I will not cease to provide for her". Even today Christians are inclined to take literally what applies to them, but the Word concerning Israel is spiritualized. When we read Luke 1:32 we agree that Jesus was born and is called the Son of the Highest. The second part of the same verse, however, *" . . . and the Lord God shall give unto him the throne of his father David"* seems to be more questionable and so it is spiritualized. The same thing happens with Zephaniah 3:12-13 for these verses are also applied literally to Israel, *"I will also leave in the midst of thee an afflicted and poor people, and they shall trust in the name of the Lord. The remnant of Israel shall not do iniquity, nor speak lies; neither shall a deceitful tongue be found in their mouth: for they shall feed and lie down, and none shall make them afraid"*. Verse 14, on the other hand, is proclaimed in the Church, *"Sing, O daughter of Zion; shout, O Israel; be glad and rejoice with all the heart, O daughter of Jerusalem"*. This has nothing to do with the Church of Jesus Christ, however. These last sentences are also meant for Israel.

We have gone into this in detail so that it becomes quite clear in our hearts that we may expect the coming Kingdom of God to be something visible and tangible, as also the return of Jesus, for it is written, *" . . . and every eye shall see Him"*.

The question now remains, who will take part in this reign of peace? Mankind will be divided into two groups; one will take part in the first resurrection, the other in the second. Everything depends upon your taking part in the first resurrection, as it says in Revelation 20:6a, *"Blessed and holy is he that hath part in the first resurrection"*. Let us prove ourselves in the light of Revelation 20 and see which group we belong to, because in verse 5 it says, *"The rest of the dead lived not again until the thousand years were finished"*. Whoever has no part in the first resurrection remains in the grave, in Hades, the realm of the dead. Those who have part in the first resurrection though, will be blessed and holy, and will experience what the

Lord has promised in Revelation 20:6b, "On such the second death hath no power, but they shall be priests of God and of Christ, and shall reign with him a thousand years". The first resurrection is the rapture. "And the dead in Christ shall rise first: then we which are alive and remain shall be caught up together with them in the clouds, to meet the Lord in the air" (1 Thessalonians 4:16b-17). We also read of this in 1 Corinthians 15, Let us take this to heart, "Blessed and holy is he that hath part in the first resurrection". These are the born-again believers who followed the Lord with all their hearts. The others will have to wait a thousand years and after this will have to appear before God for the final judgment, "And I saw the dead, small and great, stand before God . . ." (Revelation 20:12). After a thousand years the devil will be allowed to deceive one more time, but then he will meet his end, "And when the thousand years are expired, Satan shall be loosed out of his prison, and shall go out to deceive the nations which are in the four quarters of the earth . . . " (Revelation 20:7-8a). This is followed by the second resurrection. "And I saw a great white throne, and him that sat on it, from whose face the earth and the heaven fled away; and there was found no place for them. And I saw the dead, small and great, stand before God; and the books were opened: and another book was opened, which is the book of life: and the dead were judged out of those things which were written in the books, according to their works. And the sea gave up the dead which were in it; and death and hell delivered up the dead which were in them" (Revelation 20:11-13a). Many people want to be cremated out of fear. They imagine they can destroy completely everything pertaining to their existence, but they are in error. *"And death and hell delivered up the dead which were in them: and they were judged every man according to their works. And death and hell were cast into the lake of fire. This is the second death"* (Revelation 20:13b-14). This is the death which does not kill, the 'being separated from God' for all eternity. *"And whosoever was not found written in the book of life was cast into the lake of fire"* (Revelation 20:15). Something is missing at this last judgment before the great white throne. It is the Lamb and His shed blood! Forgiveness is no longer possible. That is why NOW is the time to attain the four signs that are necessary in order to take part in the first resurrection:

— Let yourself be cleansed more and more deeply, *"And every man that hath this hope in him purifieth himself, even as he is pure"* (John 3:3).
— Follow after holiness, for *"without holiness no man shall see the Lord"* (Hebrews 12:14).
— Be prepared to suffer, for *"If we be dead with him, we shall also live with him: if we suffer, we shall also reign with him"* (2 Timothy 2:11-12).
— Always be waiting for the coming of the Lord Jesus. *"For our conversation is in heaven; from whence also we look for the Saviour, the Lord Jesus Christ"* (Philippians 3:20).
  "And the Spirit and the bride say, Come. Amen. Even so, come, Lord Jesus" (Revelation 22:17a & 20b).

CHAPTER 2

PALESTINE IN THE MILLENNIUM

*"In the visions of God brought he me into the land
of Israel"* (Ezekiel 40:2).

The country we are talking about was not called
Palestine originally; it was given this name by the
Gentiles. First the Greeks called it "Syria of the
Philistines" and from this word "Philistine" -
whose territory was today's Gaza Strip - the name
"Philistea" evolved. The Romans also called it
Palaestina. During the time of England's mandate
"Palestine" was the official name for the territory
which today includes Israel and parts of Jordan,
Lebanon and the former United Arab Republic.
This name was never recognized by the Jews, and
rightfully so. Many of them have fought it as a sym-
bol of foreign rule. We should never speak of
"Palestine" in Israel, because it is the anti-Semitic
name for the country which plays such a major
part in the history of God's dealings with man. The
Arabs call it "Falestin" and the members of the
terrorist movement "El Fatah" call themselves
Palestinians. What then is the actual name of this
contested and glorious land_ "Canaan" say many.
They are wrong. That was its name when the

children of Israel took possession of it, under the leadership of Joshua, but also in Abraham's time when, under the guidance of his old father Terah, he departed from Ur. *"And Terah took Abram his son, and Lot the son of Haran his son's son, and Sarai his daughter in law, his son Abram's wife; and they went forth with them from Ur of the Chaldees, to go into the land of Canaan"* (Genesis 11:31). The Lord Himself, however, speaks over and again of "this land", for instance in Genesis 13:15 or 12:7, *"And the Lord appeared unto Abram, and said, Unto thy seed will I give this land"*. Later on the Lord often calls it "my land", through the mouth of the prophets. The name Canaan comes from the eldest son of Ham, whose father Noah, cursed Ham because of his sin. *"And Noah awoke from his wine, and knew what his younger son had done unto him. And he said, Cursed be Canaan; a servant of servants shall he be unto his brethren. And he said, Blessed be the Lord God or Shema and Canaan shall be his servant"* (Genesis 9:24-26).

During the English mandate we find in official Hebrew documents the term "Palatina E.I.". The letters "E.I." stand for "Eretz Israel". We find this "E.I." mentioned frequently in the Bible also, for instance in 2 Chronicles 2:16, *"And Solomon numbered all the strangers that were in the land of ISRAEL"*. And in Ezekiel 11:17, *"Therefore say, Thus saith the Lord God; I will even gather you from the people, and assemble you out of the countries where ye have been scattered, and I will give you the land of ISRAEL"*. From this text we learn that for God the people and land of Israel are inseparable. They not only have the same name but the same promises and both are experiencing the fulfilment of the Word of God. We can see this today, for the resurrection of Israel as a nation goes hand in hand with the resurrection of the land of Israel. The political borders of the land remained indefinite as long as Israel was not there. Under King David and Solomon the contours of the borders became ever clearer and they were just as God had promised them to Abraham's seed. *"Every place whereon the soles of your feet shall tread shall be yours: from the wilderness and Lebanon, from the river, the river Euphrates, even unto the uttermost sea shall your coast be. There shall no man be able to stand before you: for the Lord your God shall lay the fear of you and the dread of you upon all the land that ye shall tread upon, as he hath said unto you"* (Deuteronomy 11:24-25). Compare also Genesis 15:18. The same thing is promised again to Joshua, Moses' successor, *"Every place that the sole of your foot shall tread upon, that have I given unto you, as I said unto Moses. From the wilderness and this Lebanon even unto the great river, the river Euphrates, all the land of the Hittites, and unto the great sea toward the going down of the sun, shall be your coast. There shall not any man be able to stand before thee all the days of thy life"* (Joshua 1:3-5a). This is also a wonderful promise which is being fulfilled today.

The Lord also wants to extend YOUR borders. He wants to lead you out of your narrow selfish life into wide, open spaces. Begin to pray to the Lord and cry to Him like Jabez, *"And Jebez called on the God of Israel, saying, Oh that thou wouldest bless me indeed, and enlarge my coast, and that thine hand might be with me, and that thou wouldest keep me from evil, that it may not grieve me! And God granted him that which he requested"* (1 Chronicles 4:10). God's promises for His redeemed are unlimited. A great land lies before you which you should possess.

Another thing strikes us: the land of Israel always became desolate when the nation was stubborn and disobedient. *"And it shall come to pass, if ye shall hearken diligently unto my commandments which I command you this day, to love the Lord your God and to serve him with all your heart and with all your soul, that I will give you the rain of your land in his due season, the first rain and the latter rain, that thou mayest gather in thy corn, and thy wine, and thine oil. Take heed to yourselves, that your heart be not deceived, and ye turn aside, and serve other gods, and worship them; and then the Lord's wrath be kindled against you, and he shut up the heaven, that there be no rain, and that the land yield not her fruit; and lest ye perish quickly from off the good land which the Lord giveth you"* (Deuteronomy 11:13-14 & 16-17). But when Israel turned to her God again, the land and the desert blossomed again, *"And they shall build the old wastes, they shall raise up the former desolations, and they shall repair the waste cities, the desolations of many generations"* (Isaiah 61:4). According to the measure of obedience of the people, the land was blessed. This also applies to our faith-lives. According to the measure of your obedience, the Lord will bless the fields of your life with the first rain and the latter rain. Moses calls to the people, *"Therefore shall ye lay up these my words in your heart and in your soul, and bind them for a sign upon your hand, that they may be as frontlets between your eyes"* (Deuteronomy 11:18). What he means is, Don't forget this! As long as Arabs, Turks, Romans and other nations ruled the land of Israel, it was nothing but desert and malaria-infested swamps, but as soon as Israel began to return the deserts began to blossom again. We see this with our own eyes today. How much more will this be evident in the millennium when all Israel will be saved! The Scriptures describe this for us, *"If ye walk in my statutes, and keep my commandments, and do them; then I will give you rain in due season, and the land shall yield her increase, and the trees of the field shall yield their fruit. And your threshing shall reach unto the vintage, and the vintage shall reach unto the sowing time: and ye shall eat your bread to the full, and dwell in your land safely. And I will give peace in the land, and ye shall lie down, and none shall make you afraid: and I will rid evil beasts out of the land, neither shall the sword go through your land"* (Leviticus 26:3-6). An agricultural miracle will take place. There will be unceasing fertility and there will be no more fear because the Prince of peace will reign.

Let us apply this personally: as long as the "Turks and Romans" rule your land, your heart, it will remain an arid desert, but when Jesus Christ rules in you as King the Word applies to you, *"Remem-*

ber ye not the former things, neither consider the things of old. Behold, I will do a new thing; now it shall spring forth; shall ye not know it? I will even make a way in the wilderness, and rivers in the desert" (Isaiah 43:18-19). And Isaiah 58:11 says, "And the Lord shall guide thee continually, and satisfy thy soul in drought, and make fat thy bones: and thou shalt be like a watered garden, and like a spring of water, whose waters fail not". These are promises for the land and people of Israel. They show how the Lord calls the people and the land one. How wonderful that we Gentiles, who have believed in Jesus Christ, may receive these promises in our hearts that are desolate and barren as long as we live in disobedience. It also applies to us, as Jesus has promised, that streams of living water will flow from us when we believe on Him as the Scriptures say.

The Scriptures show us something quite different also, namely an absolute dependence of the land, Israel, on God the Lord, "For the land, whither thou goest in to possess it, is not as the land of Egypt, from whence ye came out, where thou sowedst thy seed, and wateredst it with thy foot, as a garden of herbs: but the land, whither ye go to possess it, is a land of hills and valleys, and drinketh water of the rain of heaven: a land which the Lord thy God careth for: the eyes of the Lord thy God are always upon it, from the beginning of the year even unto the end of the year" (Deuteronomy 11:10-12). Here the difference is stressed between the land of Israel and all other lands. But the people of Israel are also God's special property, "Now therefore, if ye will obey *my voice indeed, and keep my covenant, then ye shall be a peculiar treasure unto me above all people"* (Exodus 19:5). This special position of the land and the people is already visible now; how much more will it be in the millennium! Read carefully the words of Leviticus 26. They had to take possession of this land, this special land, by means of military force. Today also, Israel has to take possession of her land using military force.

This is a fact that many Christians cannot understand, but it remains nevertheless and as a result the millennium will not only be an agricultural miracle but also a military one. We read in Leviticus 26:7-9, *"And ye shall chase your enemies, and they shall fall before you by the sword. And five of you shall chase an hundred, and an hundred of you shall put ten thousand to flight: and your enemies shall fall before you by the sword. For I will have respect unto you, and make you fruitful, and multiply you, and establish my covenant with you".* The greatest miracle of victory over the enemy will take place in Eretz Israel at the beginning of the millennium although Israel's military position will look desperate. At this time, however, Israel's breakthrough to Jesus the Messiah will be imminent. In answer to Israel's crying and lamenting Jesus Christ will suddenly appear and consume the enemy with the spirit of His mouth (2 Thessalonians 2:8). The victory will not be accomplished by means of military power but the Spirit of the Lord will do it (Zechariah 4:6). Another characteristic to be found in Israel is her homesickness which is being healed, No other nation ever longed so much for her homeland as Israel. For two thousand years the believing Jews all over the world prayed, Lord, let Jerusalem be built again! and; Next year in Jerusalem! It is strange that it should be Israel's enemies who helped to increase the homesickness in the hearts of Jews all over the world so that since the six-day-war they are just pouring into the land. Since then worldwide Judaism identifies itself more than ever before with the Jewish state. Even before the end of the fighting crowds of enthusiastic young people arrived in Zion. The longing for peace and for home are two characteristics of the Jewish soul. The longing for home is satisfied as soon as they return to the land of their fathers. Israel is growing; day by day ships and planes from all over the world bring Jews to the Jewish state, not as tourists but as new citizens of the Holy Land.

The longing for peace in Israel is also very strong. They do not want war but ask for peace negotiations. This longing for peace, however, will only be fully satisfied when the millennium dawns. Then Isaiah 54:7-10and 13 will be fulfilled - that Word which we rightfully apply to us who believe in Jesus Christ but which we often forget is firstly meant for Israel, *"For a small moment have I forsaken thee; but with great mercies will I gather thee. In a little wrath I hid my face from thee for a moment; but with everlasting kindness will I have mercy on thee, saith the Lord thy Redeemer. For this is as the waters of Noah unto me: for as I have sworn that the waters of Noah should no more go over the earth; so have I sworn that I would not be wroth with thee, nor* rebuke thee. *For the mountains shall depart, and the hills be removed; but my kindness shall not depart from thee, neither shall the covenant of my peace be removed, saith the Lord that hath mercy on thee. . . And all thy children shall be taught of the Lord; and great shall be the peace of thy children".* That is the millenium. Israel has so many glorious promises, for instance, "The ransomed of the Lord shall return, and come to Zion with songs and everlasting joy upon their heads: they shall obtain joy and gladness and sorrow and sighing shall flee away" (Isaiah 35:10). The same things is said almost word for word in Isaiah 51:11 and again in Jeremiah 31:9, *"They shall come with weeping, and with supplications will I lead them: I will cause them to walk by the rivers of waters in a straight way, wherein they shall not stumble: for I am a father to Israel, and Ephraim is my firstborn".* This is a wonderful promise for the children of God who long for the heavenly Eretz Israel. "Blessed are they who long for Home, for their longing shall be satisfied"! The Lord Jesus has gone before us and has said that He is preparing a place for us (John 14:2), but we are not home yet. Let us return to Israel now. The identification, the oneness, of the land and people of Israel is very moving. Two prophetic statements confirm this, *"Therefore thus saith the Lord God; Now will I bring again the captivity of Jacob, and have mercy upon the whole house of Israel, and will be jealous for my holy name"* (Ezekiel 39:25). For centuries the nation of Israel was in the captivity of the powerful nations of this earth. Her land was trodden underfoot, profaned and laid waste. But again the Lord says concerning the land,

"For I will cause to return the captivity of the land, as at the first, saith the Lord" (Jeremiah 33:11b). What a privilege to be living at a time when God is fulfilling all this!

God also thought of Israel's great immigration problem, for He says, "But ye, O mountains of Israel, ye shall shoot forth your branches, and yield your fruit to my people of Israel; for they are at hand to come. For, behold, I am for you, and I will turn unto you, and ye shall be tilled and sown: and I will multiply men upon you, all the house of Israel, even all of it: and the cities shall be inhabited, and the wastes shall be builded: and I will multiply upon you man and beast; and they shall increase and bring fruit: and I will settle you after your old estates, and will do better unto you than at your beginnings: and ye shall know that I am the Lord" (Ezekiel 36:8-11). The immigration quota is rising steadily. The Soviet Union has to let more and more Jews emigrate to Israel. Professor Zand, a Jew who returned home to Israel from Russia, said that there are not 2-1/2 million Jews in Russia but 4 million.

More promises began to be fulfilled in 1967, after the six-day-war. "The Lord God which gathereth the outcasts of Israel saith, Yet will I gather others to him, beside those that are gathered unto him" (Isaiah 56:8). It must be made quite clear, however, that the complete fulfillment will only take place at the beginning of the millennium, that is at that moment when Israel will be cleansed of her sins through her conversion.

When Israel has returned home, she will come to herself like the prodigal son, through the Lord's continual blessings on her, and this before her conversion, *"And I will multiply the fruit of the tree, and the increase of the field, that ye shall receive no more reproach of famine among the heathen. Then shall ye remember your own evil ways, and your doings that were not good, and shall lothe yourselves in your own sight for your iniquities and for your abominations. Not for your sakes do I this, saith the Lord God, be it known unto you: be ashamed and confounded for your own ways, O house of Israel"* (Ezekiel 36:30-32). This is not Israel's conversion though. The full blessing will come when their change of heart has taken place. *"Thus saith the Lord God; In the day that I shall have cleansed you from all your iniquities I will also cause you to dwell in the cities, and the wastes shall be builded. And the desolate land shall be tilled, whereas it lay desolate in the sight of all that passed by. And they shall say, This land that was desolate is become like the garden of Eden; and the waste and desolate and ruined cities are become fenced, and are inhabited. Then the heathen that are left round about you shall know that I the Lord build the ruined places, and plant that that was desolate: I the Lord have spoken it, and I will do it"* (Ezekiel 36:33-36). First there is conviction of sin and then conversion. This also applies to us. The Lord does not pour out His blessing on you according to your conviction of sin and shame, but through cleansing in the precious blood of Jesus on the basis of your repentance. A revival among us Gentile Christians is desperately needed. When Israel is saved it will be too late for us, because our time will be up. In this connection I must emphasize another well-known fact: Eretz Israel will be the center of the earth in the millennium. Geographically speaking, this is already the case now, for it is the meeting point of three continents: Europe, Asia and Africa. The prophet Ezekiel saw this, *"Thus saith the Lord God; This is Jerusalem: I have set it in the midst of the nations and countries that are round about her"* (Ezekiel 5:5). Israel and the city of Jerusalem will also be the economic center of the earth. The Scriptures tell us, *"And it shall be in that day, that living waters shall go out from Jerusalem; half of them toward the former sea, and half of them toward the hinder sea: in summer and in winter shall it be. And the Lord shall be king over all the earth"* (Zechariah 14:8-9a). Through the living waters which will flow from Jerusalem, there will be great fertility, which will have mighty results in the economic field.

Jerusalem will also be the spiritual center of the world. We learn this from Micah 4:1-2, *"But in the last days it shall come to pass, that the mountain of the house of the Lord shall be established in the top of the mountains, and it shall be exalted above the hills; and people shall flow unto it. And many nations shall come, and say, Come, and let us go up to the mountain of the Lord, and to the house of the God of Jacob; and he will teach us of his ways, and we will walk in his paths: for the law shall go forth of Zion, and the word of the Lord from Jerusalem"*.

Politically and militarily speaking, Israel will also

be the center, because the Lord will be King (Zechariah 14:9). In the prophet Micah we read, *"And he shall judge among many people, and rebuke strong nations afar off; and they shall beat their swords into plowshares, and their spears into pruninghooks: nation shall not lift up a sword against nation, neither shall they learn war any more"* (Micah 4:3).

One of the most glorious miracles which will take place in the land of Israel during the millennium will be a change in the vegetation. The earth will yield fir trees instead of thorns, as it is written in Isaiah 55:13, *"Instead of the thorn shall come up the fir tree, and instead of the brier shall come up the myrtle tree: and it shall be to the Lord for a name, for an everlasting sign that shall not be cut off"*. This is the result of Calvary, for once God had to curse the earth and say, *"Thorns also and thistles shall it bring forth to thee"*. But Jesus wore a crown of thorns; He became a curse for our sakes and for Israel's sake. This is why the thorns will disappear in Israel during the millennium and in their place fragrant fir trees will grow and myrtle trees instead of the brier. That which was dead will come to life. The Dead Sea will even be healed, we read in Ezekiel 47:8-9, *"These waters issue out toward the east country, and go down into the desert, and go into the sea: which being brought forth into the sea, the waters shall be healed. And it shall come to pass, that every thing that liveth, which moveth, shall live: and there shall be a very great multitude of fish, because these waters shall come thither: for they shall be healed; and every thing shall live whether the river cometh"*.

This will all be fulfilled! Today no-one can drink the water of the Dead Sea without dying, but these waters will be healed!

All this has much to say to us and I would like to ask you, Has the curse in your life been turned into blessing through the Lord Jesus Christ? Are the prickly thorns of your proud ego, your accursed old nature, been turned into fragrant fir trees? What is the center of your life? Is it Jesus? Just as the land and nation of Israel will become one with the King, so you also should be one in body, soul and spirit with the Lord Jesus Christ. We do not have much time for He is coming soon. Therefore, he that hath ears to hear let him hear what the Spirit saith to the Churches!

CHAPTER 3

ISRAEL'S NATIONAL AND SPIRITUAL FUTURE

"There is neither Jew nor Greek, there is neither bond nor free, there is neither male nor female: for ye are all one in Christ Jesus" (Galatians 3:28).

"I say then, Hath God cast away his people? God forbid. For I also am an Israelite, of the seed of Abraham, of the tribe of Benjamin" (Romans 11:1).

The word "Israel" occurs about seventy times in the New Testament, and it is used not in a spiritual sense but literally. In our days there are many Christian adversaries who vehemently deny Israel's future. This attitude, which is typical of thousands of Christians, is expressed in a letter I received recently from Paris. I mention this letter because it represents many others which were also written in a similar manner. The writer in question supposes that Israel has not been given any promise of restoration because she rejected the Saviour. With the crucifixion Israel lost her position as God's chosen people for ever and could no longer be His means of bringing salvation to the world. Apparently the writer has overlooked Romans chapter

11 and never noticed that it is Israel's temporary casting away which is the reconciling of the world (Romans 11:15). The Christian-camouflaged anti-Semitism quotes as proof the above text, *"There is neither Jew nor Greek, there is neither bond nor free, there is neither male nor female: for ye are all one in Christ Jesus"* (Galatians 3:28). This is a glorious truth! These words speak of the organic, indivisble unity of the Church of Jesus Christ. The Denominations, Churches and fellowships are split up into organizations, but not, however, the body of Jesus Christ, which is an organism. This Bible verse does not say that a Jew who is converted to Jesus Christ ceases to be a Jew. If that were so, then, according to Galatians 3:28, a man would cease to be a man and a woman would no longer be a woman, a servant no longer a servant and a free man no longer free. The differences mentioned in this text between Jews, Greeks, etc., do not cease to exist as such, but they have nothing to do with the spiritual unity and the spiritual advantages of the one over the other. It is said that the word "Jew" occurs about two hundred times in the Bible; I have counted two hundred and thirty times. This word "Jew" is always used in the Bible in contrast to the word "Gentile". "Jerusalem" occurs in the Bible more than one hundred and forty times, always being referred to as the capital of Judaea, that is Israel, except where the Scriptures expressly refer to the heavenly or new Jerusalem from above. These explanations show us the difference between Israel's position and the position of the Church of Jesus Christ in God's plan of salvation. The following question is of tremendous importance: If Ishmael and Isaac are both sons of

Abraham, have they also the same inheritance and the same promises? No, only one is heir: Isaac! (Genesis 15:4 and Genesis 17:18 & 21). In the same way, the natural nation of Israel and the spiritual one, that is the believers - Jews and Gentiles -, both belong to Abraham's seed. Like Isaac and Ishmael, however, they do not have the same promises, the same inheritance nor the same future. Although Jews and Gentiles have the same position in the Church of Jesus Christ and as members of the Church, according to Colossians 3:11, they are spiritually molded together, - *"Where there is neither Greek nor Jew, circumcision nor uncircumcision, Barbarian, Scythian, bond nor free: but Christ is all, and in all"* - these facts in no way annul God's special plans for Israel.

Let us now consider Israel's wonderful future. We find in the Scriptures, in connection with the nation of Israel, over and again the word "till". The Lord Jesus says, *"Behold, your house is left unto you desolate. For I say unto you, Ye shall not see me henceforth, TILL ye shall say, Blessed is he that cometh in the name in the Lord"* (Matthew 23: 38-39). This "till" still lies ahead of us. All Israel will worship and praise Him when they are converted to Him. Where the land is concerned, the "till" has already been fulfilled, as it was predicted, *"And they shall build the old wastes, they shall raise up the former desolations, and they shall repair the waste cities, the desolations of many generations. And strangers shall stand and feed your flocks, and the sons of the alien shall be your plowmen and your vine-dressers"* (Isaiah 61:4-5). There is also a wonderful, divine "till" where the city is concerned, *"And they shall fall by the edge of the sword, and shall be led away captive into all nations: and Jerusalem shall be trodden down of the Gentiles, UNTIL the times of the Gentiles be fulfilled"* (Luke 21:24).

Israel will have a national as well as a spiritual future. This will finally flow together with the Church of Jesus Christ. God's ways, however, with the Church and with Israel leading towards the one great goal, the establishment of His kingdom, are quite different. God is working visibly in and through His people by means of works and miracles now already, whereas the invisible part, the transformation of their hearts, will take place afterwards. In the Church it is just the opposite. The invisible comes first. A person who is born again is inwardly renewed through the Spirit of God and then the fruit of the Spirit becomes visible. There are two prophecies concerning Israel's future which are so clear that they cannot be made more clear and so spiritual that they cannot be made more spiritual. The first says, *"And I will plant them upon their land, and they shall no more be pulled up out of their land which I have given them, saith the Lord thy God"* (Amos 9:15). That is very plain. This promise, which refers to their earthly position, is becoming visible today in the Middle East in a mighty way before the eyes of the whole world. The other promise is in the New Testament and concerns the spiritual restoration of Israel. *"What shall the receiving of them be, but life from the dead?"* (Romans 11:15b). Just as the fulfilment of the natural promise is visible today, so the spiritual promise is also being fulfilled in

Israel! All Israel will be saved! The first signs are already appearing; an enquiring after the Messiah is audible. The prophet Ezekiel describes this procedure as follows, *"So I prophesied as I was commanded: and as I prophesied, there was a noise, and behold a shaking, and the bones came together, bone to his bone. And when I beheld, lo, the sinews and the flesh came up upon them, and the skin covered them above: but there was no breath in them"* (Ezekiel 37:7-8). This is the situation in Israel today, but the fulfillment is not yet complete, because it continues in verse 9, *"Then he said unto me, Prophesy unto the wind, prophesy, son of man, and say to the wind, Thus saith the Lord God; Come from the four winds, O breath, and breathe upon these slain, that they may live. So I prophesied as he commanded me and the breath came into them and they lived, and stood up upon their feet, an exceeding great army"* (Ezekiel 37:9-10). It becomes unmistakably clear that Israel is meant here and not the Church when we read on in verse 11, *"Then he said unto me, Son of man, these bones are the whole house of Israel: behold, they say, Our bones are dried, and our hope is lost: we are cut off for our parts"*. Many Christians can follow thus far, but the text continues, *"Therefore prophesy and say unto them, Thus saith the Lord God; Behold, O my people, I will open your graves, and cause you to come up out of your graves, and bring you into the land of Israel. And ye shall know that I am the Lord, when I have opened your graves, O my people, and brought you up out of your graves, and shall put my spirit in you, and ye shall live"* (Ezekiel 37:12-14a). In this chapter the wonderful sequence of events in the nation of Israel is portrayed for us and we are shown that the national and then also the spiritual future will be fulfilled. We read in verses 25 and 27 of the same chapter, *"And they shall dwell in the land that I have given unto Jacob my servant, wherein your fathers have dwelt; and they shall dwell therein, even they and their children, and their children's children for ever: and my servant David shall be their prince for ever. . . My tabernacle also shall be with them: yea, I will be their God, and they shall be my people".* Thus we have first the return of the nation to the land (the national future) and then the conversion of the nation (the spiritual future). From this we see clearly that not only the national prophecies will be fulfilled but also the spiritual ones. In this way the Lord fulfills His wonderful promises, one after the other.

Abraham was told by the Lord, *"Arise, walk through the land in the length of it and in the breadth of it; for I will give it unto thee"* (Genesis 13:17). Abraham traveled through the arena of the old Orient in those days and touched all those lands whose rulers later affected the history of God's covenant people. This included the whole of Mesopotamia, present-day Iraq, to the country of the Nile, Egypt. In that Abraham obediently walked through the land in its length and breadth - the Lord did not yet mention the height and depth - Abraham, a man of the Advent acted in accordance with the Spirit of Jesus and rejoiced to see from afar, *". . .to comprehend with all the saints what is the breadth, and length, and depth, and height; and to know the love of Christ, which passeth* knowledge, that ye might be filled with all the fulness of God" (Ephesians 3:18). If, as mentioned above, Abraham only travelled the horizontal line, by the grace of God, we also know the vertical one. This verticle line, from heaven to earth, found its fulfillment in Jesus' death on the cross and in His cry, "It is finished!" There heaven and earth united, and this happened in Israel! I repeat, not only the horizontal line but also the vertical line was drawn. God will establish the reign of Jesus Christ from heaven together with the glorified Church. This concerns the Church now, but let us turn back to the coming worldwide rule of Israel and to her position in the Kingdom of Jesus Christ. When Israel's national, international and spiritual calling all co-incide this will be an indescribable blessing for the whole world. "Now if the fall of them be the riches of the world, and the diminishing of them the riches of the Gentiles; how much more their fulness" (Romans 11:12). All nations will then rejoice over the divine government through Israel. Psalm 67:3-4 says in this connection, "Let the people praise thee, O God; let all the people praise thee. O let the nations be glad and sing for joy: for thou shalt judge the people righteously, and govern the nations upon earth". According to Psalm 18:43, Israel will become the head of the nations, "Thou hast delivered me from the strivings of the people; and thou hast made me the head of the heathen: a people I have not known shall serve me". God also promised Moses this. "And it shall come to pass, if thou shalt hearken diligently unto the voice of the Lord thy God to observe and to do all his commandments which I command thee this day, that the Lord thy

God will set thee on high above all nations of the earth" (Deuteronomy 28:1). Many will object here, But Israel isn't obedient yet! Indeed, until now the Lord has only been able to fulfill His natural promise to Israel but not His spiritual promise. Why not? Has Israel not suffered enough yet? The cause lies with the Gentiles and Gentile Christians. These are not yet spiritually obedient, and therefore Israel is still blind to her Messiah, *"Blindness in part is happened to Israel, UNTIL the fulness of the Gentiles be come in"* (Romans 11:25). The blindness will not leave Israel until the last Gentile is converted, until the fulness of the Gentiles be come in. Therefore whoever judges Israel judges himself. A mighty revival amongst us would soon bring about the fulness of the Gentiles and Israel's blindness would be lifted. Not only the nations as such have sinned against Israel from a psychical, political, economic and military point of view, but far more, Christianity is guilty towards Israel through her indolence, prayerlessness and spiritual fruitlessness. Therefore we call upon every child of God to, "Awake, you who sleep, and arise from the dead, so that Christ can give you light and He can appear in Israel"

How we, the Gentiles are hindering the fulfillment of God's plan for us (the gentiles) ~ but more significantly the against Israel. We sure need revival

CHAPTER 4

ISRAEL'S POSITION IN THE MILLENNIUM

*"For if the casting away of them be the recon-
ciling of the world, what shall the receiving of
them be, but life from the dead?"* (Romans 11:15).

When Israel is converted the outer shell of this
people will suddenly fall away. The two thousand
year-old puzzle will be solved when Jesus, the
Messiah, reveals Himself to His brothers, as Joseph
once revealed himself to his brothers. There seems
to be no answer to the question, "What is Israel?"
"Why did this nation have to go through such
terrible suffering?" or "Why is she rejected by all
nations?" The answer will only be given when her
Messiah appears and His wonderful resurrection
power is united with His resurrected people. Then
we shall have the literal fulfillment of that which
the prophet Micah prophesied, *"And he shall
stand and feed in the strength of the Lord, in the
majesty of the name of the Lord his God; and they
shall abide: for now shall he be great unto the
ends of the earth. And the remnant of Jacob shall
be among the Gentiles in the midst of many*

people as a dew from the Lord, as the showers upon the grass, that tarrieth not for man, nor waiteth for the sons of men" (Micah 5:4 & 7). Israel will then no longer depend on the support of the U.S.A. or any other nation, but Jesus Christ, the Messiah Himself, will be her greatness, power and glory. Although Israel will have political, military and economic predominance, this will all be of no importance in comparison with the inconceivable glory which Isaiah attempts to describe in Isaiah 60:3, "And the Gentiles shall come to thy light, and kings to the brightness of thy rising". Then the "worm Jacob", as Israel is called in Isaiah 41:14, will be the head of all nations. "And all people of the earth shall see that thou art called by the name of the Lord; and they shall be afraid of thee. And the Lord shall make thee the head, and not the tail; and thou shalt be above only, and thou shalt not be beneath; if that thou hearken unto the commandments of the Lord thy God, which I command thee this day, to observe and to do them" (Deuteronomy 28:10 & 13). Is this not also the secret of the glory of a child of God here on earth? What is your position without Jesus? Weak, miserable, despondent, sinful, unhappy and un-faithful! And what are you with Jesus? Glorious and righteous, blameless and victorious! This will be reality at the moment of the rapture when we see Him as He is and are united with Him. The dawning of this thousand-year, unspeakably glorious reign of peace is imminent. The con-sequence for all nations will be joy but also fear, "O clap your hands, all ye people; shout unto God with the voice of triumph. For the Lord most high is terrible; he is a great King over all the earth. He

"But they shall sit every man under his vine and under his fig tree; and none shall make them afraid; for the mouth of the Lord of hosts hath spoken it" (Micah 4:4).

shall subdue the people under us, and the nations under our feet. He shall choose our inheritance for us, the excellency of Jacob whom he loved" (Psalm 47:1-4). Not everyone will submit themselves unconditionally to the Lordship of Jesus Christ, but those who resist will inevitably have to reckon with judgment which will proceed from Israel, *"For the nation and kingdom that will not serve thee shall perish; yea, those nations shall be utterly wasted"* (Isaiah 60:12). At this time the chronic crisis in Lebanon will also be solved, *"The glory of Lebanon shall come unto thee, the fir tree, the pine tree, and the box together, to beautify the place of my sanctuary; and I will make the place of my feet glorious"* (Isaiah 60:13). All these statements of Scripture are in accordance with God's original intentions for Israel. He is realizing everything which He planned before the foundation of the world. We also read in Deuteronomy 32:8-9 that all nations will be subordinate to Israel, *"When the Most High divided to the nations their inheritance, when he separated the sons of Adam, he set the bounds of the people according to the number of the children of Israel. For the Lord's portion is his people; Jacob is the lot of his inheritance".*

What are the consequences for us Gentile Christians who are living at the time when this is all beginning to take place?

1. Bless Israel and Jerusalem, for the Lord said to the father of Israel, "I will bless them that bless thee, and curse him that curseth thee".

2. If you are a child of God, it is important that you prepare yourself for your sudden departure, because the rapture is imminent. When the Church is raptured the Antichrist will be able to rage for a short time, but then the millennium will begin.

3. Now that the night is far spent and tribulations are increasingly stronger hold fast to Jesus and remain crucified with Him until He comes. Through the obedience in faith, unite yourself with the Holy Spirit so that you can call with the Spirit, *"Come quickly, Lord Jesus".*

Inded, come quickly ~ things are getting so tough already ~ what with rampant sin, violence, drunkeness, inflation, inability to do anything to improve the world, till You, Lord Jesus come

CHAPTER 5

THE POSITION OF THE CHURCH NOW AND IN THE MILLENNIUM

"To the intent that now unto the principalities and powers in heavenly places might be known by the church the manifold wisdom of God" (Ephesians 3:10).

God has a future planned for the Church of Jesus Christ. In order to understand this future better, let us first examine His plan for the Church at this time. Ephesians 3:10 tells of this, *"To the intent that now unto the principalities and powers in heavenly places might be known by the church the manifold wisdom of God"*. That is a tremendous statement! How can we speak befittingly of the manifold wisdom of God? Paul says, *"This is a great mystery: but I speak concerning Christ and the church"* (Ephesians 5:32). With this he indicates that the Church is an object of God's unfathomable, all-embracing wisdom. The Amplified Bible formulates this text as follows: *"The purpose is that through the church the complicated, many-sided wisdom of God in all its infinite variety and innumerable aspects might now be made known to the angelic rulers and authorities (principalities and powers) in the heavenly sphere"*. The inexhaustible wisdom of God finds its expression in the Church, in that children of Satan become children of God. These many members become a body, for God's beloved Son forms an organic unity with His blood-bought ones, of whom He is the head. The angel world marvels at this, while Satan gnashes his teeth. Our spiritual minds make us strangers in this world and we must be preserved as such. Peter says in this connection, *"Dearly beloved, I beseech you as strangers and pilgrims, abstain from fleshly lusts, which war against the soul"* (1 Peter 2:11). We understand, therefore, the reason for the many trials and temptations, for we represent here on earth and before the invisible world a part of the manifold glory and wisdom of God.

What is God's plan for the Church in the future? Ephesians 2:7 gives us the answer, *"That in the ages to come he might shew the exceeding riches of his grace in his kindness toward us through Christ Jesus"*. The Amplified Bible translates this verse, *"He did this that He might clearly demonstrate through the ages to come the immeasurable riches of His free grace in kindness and goodness of heart toward us in Christ Jesus"*.

The revelation of the exceeding riches of His grace is so unimaginably great that we can only perceive something of it when we consider the seven pictures of the Church which the Lord Jesus has given us:

1. We are the sheep of one Shepherd — Jesus.

2. We are living stones, built up into a spiritual house on the one foundation — Jesus.

3. We are branches of one vine — Jesus Christ.

4. We are members of one body — Jesus Christ.

5. We are priests in the Holy of Holies, — through Jesus Christ.

6. We are shining lights in the darkness — through Jesus Christ.

7. We are the bride of the Bridegroom — Jesus.

We see from this that it is a great mystery. For this reason we long for the fulfillment of the words, *"When Christ, who is our life, shall appear, then shall ye also appear with him in glory"* (Colossians 3:4). This glory Jesus wants to give us. He expressed this in His High-Priestly prayer, *"Father, I will that they also, whom thou hast given me, be with me where I am; that they may behold my glory, which thou hast given me: for thou lovedst me before the foundation of the world"* (John 17:24). From these words of the Lord we see that the inconceivable glory of the Church is connected with the love of the Father for the Son and the love of the Son for the Church.

The Church and Israel are organs of salvation which are both closely connected with the coming Kingdom, the millennium. Many people believe that the Church is the spiritual continuation of Israel. In other words, Israel has been rejected forever as God's means of salvation and the Church has become her successor. Therefore all God's promises to Israel have been transferred to the Church who has in this way taken over the inheritance of Israel. This is a satanic lie! The Church is not Israel's successor but a spiritual link between the rejection and re-acceptance of Israel. These two organs of salvation are united with one another in Jesus Christ. The Lord Jesus told His disciples that He would build His Church but also that He would appoint His Kingdom. When Peter confessed, *"Thou art the Christ, the Son of the living God"*, the Lord said to him, *"Thou art Peter, and upon this rock I will build my church; and the gates of hell shall not prevail against it"* (Matthew 16:18). In the same way He speaks also of His Kingdom, however, *"And I appoint unto you a kingdom, as my Father hath appointed unto me"* (Luke 22:29). Or as James says, *"God at first did visit the Gentiles, to take out of them a people for his name. After this I will return, and will build again the tabernacle of David, which is fallen down; and I will build again the ruins thereof, and I will set it up"* (Acts 15:14 & 16). We can see this parallel today in Israel and in the Church. The Church of Jesus Christ is being built at a time when Satan is able to exercise unlimited power on earth; but the Church cannot be overcome by him because one day she will reign. What a great miracle we have before our very eyes! While the devil goes around like a roaring lion, the Church is being built. The power of the kingdom will be exercised, however, during the time when Satan is bound for a thousand years. Revelation 20:2 speaks of the twelve apostles who were persecuted by

"He that believeth on me, as the scripture hath said, out of his belly shall flow rivers of living water" (John 7:28).

Satan but afterwards sit on twelve thrones to judge the twelve tribes of Israel. This is also a picture of the Church, for Jesus said to His disciples, *"Verily I say unto you, That ye which have followed me, in the regeneration when the Son of man shall sit in the throne of his glory, ye also shall sit upon twelve thrones, judging the twelve tribes of Israel"* (Matthew 19:28). We must remember this, that the Church is the body for which the Father gave His Son Jesus as the head. Jesus Christ has been appointed King by the Father for the Kingdom. This is the fulfillment of Ephesians 1:10, *"That in the dispensation of the fullness of times he might gather together in one all things in Christ, both which are in heaven, and which are on earth; even in him"*. For a thousand years we shall have heaven on earth. After that the last thing which Peter saw with his prophetic eye will take place, *"Nevertheless we, according to his promise, look for new heavens and a new earth, wherein dwelleth righteousness"* (2 Peter 3:13). Paul, on the other hand, saw the various phases of the Kingdom, *"But every man in his own order: Christ the firstfruits; afterward they that are Christ's at his coming. Then cometh the end, when he shall have delivered up the kingdom to God, even the Father; when he shall have put down all rule and all authority and power"* (1 Corinthians 15:23-24). In this connection, I want to refer to the Lord's request, *"Thy kingdom come"*, as this is so often misunderstood. These words do not mean that through the spreading of the Gospel the reign of Christ will be brought about, for it is clear from the context of the Bible that the present proclamation of the Kingdom of heaven is an inner preparation for the coming visible Kingdom of God. We are now in God's royal school and are being humbled in order to be exalted afterwards. *"If we suffer, we shall also reign with him"* (2 Timothy 2:12a). The task of the Church until the millennial government takes over is clearly outlined by the Lord Jesus, *"And as they heard these things, he added and spake a parable, because he was nigh to Jerusalem, and because they thought that the kingdom of God should immediately appear. He said therefore, A certain nobleman went into a far country to receive for himself a kingdom, and to return. And he called his ten servants, and delivered them ten pounds, and said unto them, Occupy till I come"* (Luke 19:11-13). This is our task, *"Occupy till I come"!* We must redeem the time by praying, striving, witnessing and inviting others to hear the Word, for the Lord Jesus said, *"The Son of man is come to seek and to save that which was lost"* (Luke 19:10).

Let us remember that Israel will again be the organ of salvation on earth when the spiritual link, the Church, is removed from the earth at the rapture. In the midst of the Great Tribulation salvation will break through again from Israel. The whole world, including Israel, will experience an unprecedented measure of tribulation (Daniel 12:1, Matthew 24:21). The last battle of the nations at Armageddon will be a terrible reality (Revelation 16:16). Then, however, when Israel laments and cries to her Messiah, it will not only be the moment of deliverance but also the moment when Christ will establish His Kingdom together with those who will rule with Him for a thousand years. The Lord

Jesus Himself gives us a clear description of this, *"When the Son of man shall come in his glory, and all the holy angels with him, then shall he sit upon the throne of his glory. Then shall the King say unto them on his right hand, Come, ye blessed of my Father, inherit the kingdom prepared for you from the foundation of the world"* (Matthew 25:31 & 34).

We now come to the urgent question, Where will the Church be during the millennium? We are told in Philippians 1:23, *" . . . with Christ"*. What we now experience in spirit will then be an indescribable, blissful reality, for we shall see Him as He is. Notice the words *"with him"* which occur over and again. In the following chapter we shall go into the question of where the Church will be during the millennium more thoroughly. My question now is, Are you ready to be revealed with Him in glory, in the millennium? When Jesus departed from His disciples He said, *"Lo, I am with you always, even unto the end of the world"* (Matthew 28:20b). This means that Christ is now in us and with us through His Holy Spirit. After the rapture, however, we shall be with Christ physically and bodily. This is what 1 Thessalonians 4:17 tells us, *" . . . So shall we ever be with the Lord"*. Truly, great and wonderful mysteries! They are hidden from the world but revealed to the child of God. Nevertheless, our knowledge is in part, for the mystery of the Lord is great. The greatest mystery is Jesus Himself, *"Great is the mystery of godliness: God was manifest in the flesh"* (1 Timothy 3:16). Knowing Jesus as He is, is the most important condition for our hope for the future. Paul speaks of another mystery in 2 Thessalonians 2:7, *"For the mystery of iniquity doth already work: only he who now letteth will let, until he be taken out of the way"*. When the hindrance is removed this devilish mystery will be revealed, namely the Antichrist. A third mystery which is hidden from many Christians in our day is Israel, *"For I would not, brethren, that ye should be ignorant of this MYSTERY, lest ye should be wise in your own conceits; that blindness in part is happened to Israel, until the fullness of the Gentiles be come in"* (Romans 11:25). When we understand this mystery we also understand the mysteries of the Church. One is in Ephesians 5:32, *"This is a great mystery: but I speak concerning Christ and the church"*. We read of the other in 1 Corinthians 15:51-52a, *"Behold, I shew you a mystery; we shall not all sleep, but we shall all be changed, in a moment, in the twinkling of an eye"*. Each mystery is revealed in its own time. First Jesus revealed Himself to the world and then the Antichrist who took the place of the Lord Jesus. In our day the mystery of Israel is being revealed and finally the whole creation is waiting for the revelation of the last mystery concerning the Church, *"For the earnest expectation of the creature waiteth for the manifestation of the sons of God"* (Romans 8:19).

The way to the Kingdom of God, the millennium, is a way which is wet with tears; we must not forget this. In Acts 14:22 we read that Paul did the following, *"Confirming the souls of the disciples, and exhorting them to continue in the faith, and that we must through much tribulation enter into* the kingdom of God". Yes, the Church has a part in the sufferings of Jesus, but these are a necessary preparation for the glorious kingdom, "So that we ourselves glory in you in the churches of God for your patience and faith in all your persecutions and tribulations that ye endure: which is a manifest token of the righteous judgment of God, that ye may be counted worthy of the kingdom of God, for which ye also suffer" (2 Thessalonians 1:4-5).

CHAPTER 6

WHERE WILL THE CHURCH BE DURING THE MILLENNIUM

". . .and the dead in Christ shall rise first: then we which are alive and remain shall be caught up together with them in the clouds, to meet the Lord in the air: and so shall we ever be with the Lord" (1 Thessalonians 16b-17).

The first meeting place of Jesus with His saints at the rapture is only mentioned once in the Bible and that is in the above quoted text. We shall meet Jesus in the air and see Him as He is. The meeting place of Jesus with His people Israel, however, will be on the earth. The exact geographical place is described by the prophet Zechariah, *"And his feet shall stand in that day upon the mount of Olives. . ."* (Zechariah 14:4a). Israel is God's earthly people and the Lord Jesus will meet her on earth. The Church is His heavenly people and He will meet her in the air.

"And I saw heaven opened, and behold a white horse; and he that sat upon him was called Faithful and True, and in righteousness he doth judge and make war. And the armies which were in heaven followed him upon white horses, clothed

in fine linen, white and clean" (Revelation 19:11 &
14). This speaks of the return of the Lord Jesus in
great power and glory, accompanied by His bride,
the Church. The armies on white horses are the
Church. Even Enoch was able to see this wonderful happening in spirit, and Jude writes, *"And
Enoch also, the seventh from Adam, prophesied
of these, saying, Behold, the Lord cometh with ten
thousands of his saints"* (Jude 14). Also the
prophet Zechariah writes, *". . .and the Lord my
God shall come, and all the saints with thee"*
(Zechariah 14:5b). When this happens many
wonderful things, but also many terrible things,
will take place in heaven and on earth in quick
succession. In order to understand where the
Church will be during the millennium we must
briefly consider both the wonderful and also the
terrible things, firstly in connection with the rapture. Those people who take part in the rapture
will experience inconceivable bliss, but this sudden happening will bring indescribable despair for
those left behind and great trouble for Israel. The
tragedy for those who are left behind on earth will
be:
. . .that the physical absence of the children of God
will be a family tragedy for many thousands
because the great separation has become reality.
. . .that the Holy Spirit is no longer present on
earth and God will awaken many who did not take
heed of the word with a great shock.
. . .that the Antichrist is perceptibly present and
celebrating his satanic triumph.

We are not able to imagine this situation, but this is
what Jesus meant when He said, *"For then shall be*

*great tribulation, such as was not since the begin-
ning of the world to this time, no, nor ever shall
be"* (Matthew 24:21). We shall not go into what will
happen during the Great Tribulation on earth here,
that is, the initial enthusiasm and the worldwide
deception through the Antichrist followed by a
terrible massacre. Let us rather take note of the fact
that the Church, and therewith the Holy Spirit, is
gone from the earth and there is an immeasurable
vacuum left behind. This means that the hindrance
to the revelation of the Antichrist, the highest
potentate of wickedness, will be removed. Of this
climax of the Satanic revelation of earth, we read
in the Scriptures, *"Therefore rejoice, ye heavens,
and ye that dwell in them. Woe to the inhabiters
of the earth and of the sea! for the devil is come
down unto you, having great wrath, because he
knoweth that he hath but a short time"*
(Revelation 12:12). Thus we see, on the one hand,
utter bliss in heaven and, on the other hand, utter
despair on earth. This unprecedented situation on
earth announces the coming of Jesus, for *"the mor-
ning cometh, and also the night"* (Isaiah 21:12).

How will the Lord return after the rapture and after the Great Tribulation? Firstly, - visibly! It says
that every eye shall see Him, and in Zechariah 14:4
it says quite clearly, *". . .and his feet shall stand
upon the mount of Olives"*. Secondly, He will not
come alone and not accompanied by angels but
with His bride, the Church. What will happen
then? Will He immediately set up His thousand-
year reign of peace? No, first of all the victory of
the Lamb, together with the glorified Church will
be revealed. I want to emphasize that the important

thing is the Jurisdiction of the victory, and not the conquering of the enemy as it is often expounded. It is the victory which has long since been won which will now be revealed. Of this collision with the Antichrist it is written, *"These shall make war with the Lamb, and the Lamb shall overcome them: for he is Lord of lords, and King of kings: and they that are with him are called, and chosen, and faithful"* (Revelation 17:14). When the Lamb returns with His called and chosen ones, He will overcome the enemy because He is the Lord of all lords and King of all kings! We can see how this achieved victory is put into practice from the description of the means which the Lord uses. Bombs? No! The destruction of the enemy will take place in a completely different manner: *"And then shall that Wicked be revealed, whom the Lord shall consume with the spirit of his mouth, and shall destroy with the brightness of his coming"* (2 Thessalonians 2:8). At the return of our Lord we see His sovereignty, for He does not first have to overcome an enemy but through the breath of His mouth, through His Spirit, through His very appearing even, He will make an end of him.

Do you want to be present on that great day when the victory of the Lamb is put into practice? Then you must learn here during your life on earth to claim it in your daily life. We can and must do this! How can we do it? *"Not by might, nor by power, but by my spirit, saith the Lord of hosts"* (Zechariah 4:6). Your personality is also involved, which is to say, if you live your life walking in the light your personality is already pure victory and the devil is afraid.

Notice that the Lamb will overcome him because He HAS overcome. He only needs to appear, for wherever Jesus comes Satan's power is broken. When Jesus lives in us and He has absolute control over our lives we are invincible and our life is a life of victory. In order that we manifest visibly the victory of the Lamb before all the world at His coming, we are told to practice it now already. My question to you, my brother and my sister, is 'Do you practice this victory in your everyday life?' Time is running out! Soon you are to appear with the coming King, Jesus Christ, from the opened heavens.

Let us now consider a further aspect of the question as to where the Church will be during the millennium. *"And the glory of the Lord shall be revealed, and all flesh shall see it together: for the mouth of the Lord hath spoken it"* (Isaiah 40:5). What a piercingly clear word!

The glory of the Lord will be revealed on earth so that all flesh shall see it together. The Church of Jesus Christ has been given an express promise concerning the revelation of the glory of the Lamb, *"When Christ, who is our life, shall appear, then shall ye also appear with him in glory"* (Colossians 3:4). What is the first and foremost task of the Church at her revelation with Him in glory? Firstly the jurisdiction of the Lamb is to be exercised. The Lord Jesus Himself gives us a clear description of this in Matthew 25:31-32, *"When the Son of man shall come in his glory, and all the holy angels with him, then shall he sit upon the throne of his glory: and before him shall be*

"For as the lightning, that lighteneth out of the one part under heaven, shineth unto the other part under heaven; so shall also the Son of man be in his day." (Luke 17:24)

gathered all nations: and he shall separate them one from another, as a shepherd divideth his sheep from the goats". From these words of Jesus we can learn something which is very important for our position when we, by the grace of God, have become conquerors. Firstly, the exercising of the jurisdiction of the Lamb is a judgment on earth, for all nations must appear before Him. This is not to be confused with Revelation 20:12a, ". . .the dead, small and great, stand before God". This refers to the day of judgment. The question which the Lord will put to each nation will be "What did you do to and with Israel?" Literally, "And the King shall answer and say unto them, Verily I say unto you, Inasmuch as ye have done it unto one of the least of these my brethren, ye have done it unto me" (Matthew 25:40). The Lord Jesus will not deny His earthly nationality at the exercising of His jurisdiction. Those nations which blessed Israel are brothers of the King and will then be installed as EARTHLY heirs together with Him in His reign of peace. We read this in Matthew 25:34, "Then shall the King say unto them on his right hand, come, ye blessed of my Father, inherit the kingdom prepared for you from the foundation of the world". Notice that these do not have the same position as the Church. They are also heirs in the millennium but the Church is more.

The judgment on the enemies of Israel will be terrible! The Lord says, "Then shall he say also unto them on the left hand, Depart from me, ye cursed, into everlasting fire, prepared for the devil and his angels" (Matthew 25:41). Paul said expressly that the Church will also take part in the exercising of jurisdiction upon the nations, *"Do ye not know that the saints shall judge the world"* (1 Corinthians 6:2a). We do not hear this from the mouth of Jesus. He simply says, *"When the Son of man shall come in his glory, and all the holy angels with him, then shall he sit upon the throne of his glory"* (Matthew 25:31). Why is the Church not mentioned specifically by the Lord? I believe this is for a glorious reason: the oneness of the Church and the Lamb! The Church is then the wife of the Lamb, for the wedding of the Lamb in heaven has already taken place. The Church is simultaneously His body and His members and He is our head. The union of the Church with the Lamb is so taken for granted and so perfect that it is no longer specifically mentioned by the Lord.

After this first stage of the revelation of glory, the exercising of the jurisdiction, at the reign of peace follows. The Lord Jesus will come into power with His own. This is promised us in 2 Timothy 2:12a, *"If we suffer, we shall also reign with him"*. Amongst the four groups of believers which are described in Revelation 20 we also find in verse 4 the Church of Jesus Christ mentioned as such, *". . .and they lived and reigned with Christ a thousand years"*. The question as to where we shall be during the millennium, however, is still not quite answered. We could put the question even more plainly and ask, What will our address be during the millennium? The Lord Jesus was asked of His disciples when He lived here on earth, *"Rabbi, where dwellest thou? He saith unto them, Come and see"*, (cf. John 1:38a-39b). It is no secret where the born-again believers will be. Let us remember, ". . .*so shall we ever be with the Lord*" (1 Thessalonians 4:17b). We are closely united with the King and will share His earthly, but even more so His heavenly glory. This means that *we shall reign with Him on earth but we shall not live on earth*. The earthly Jerusalem will then experience the same as it did in Old Testament times. The Lord was at that time amongst the people of Israel in the Shekinah but He sat on His throne in heaven. The heavenly Jerusalem, according to Revelation 21:9-10, is identical with the Lamb's wife and is doubtless closely united with the earthly Jerusalem in Israel. The question of our domicile is answered even more clearly when we consider the risen Lord. He remained forty days on the earth and yet He was not on the earth. He appeared to His disciples and He disappeared again. Matter and distance were no longer a hindrance to Him. He ate with the disciples and then suddenly He was no longer there. The astonishing thing will be that we too, who are conquerors and blood-bought ones, will also receive a glorious body like His glorious body at the first resurrection. According to Philippians 3:21, this will take place *"according to the working whereby he is able even to subdue all things unto himself"*. This, my dear brethren, shows us where we shall live during the millennium. The exact address is given us in John 14:2, *"In my Father's house"*. The Lord Jesus Himself gave us this address, *"In my Father's house are many mansions"*. We shall be active on this earth, sometimes visible but often invisible like the angels, for the Lord says we shall be like the angels in the resurrection of the dead. In the millennium each one will receive a measure of government according to the measure of his faithfulness here on earth. Our home is and remains on high, however. I would like you to think on the words of our Lord Jesus now, *"To him that overcometh will I grant to sit with me in my throne, even as I also overcame, and am set down with my Father in his throne"* (Revelation 3:21).

CHAPTER 7

THE NATIONS IN THE MILLENNIUM

"Therefore wait ye upon me, saith the Lord, until the day that I rise up to the prey: for my determination is to gather the nations, that I may assemble the kingdoms, to pour upon them mine indignation, even all my fierce anger: for all the earth shall be devoured with the fire of my jealousy. For then will I turn to the people a pure language, that they may all call upon the name of the Lord, to serve him with one consent. From beyond the rivers of Ethiopia my suppliants, even the daughter of my dispersed, shall bring mine offering" (Zephaniah 3:8-10).

One of the most important characteristics of the millennium is its significance for the nations. We have already considered the position of Israel and the Church. According to Matthew 25:31, the nations will be judged by the Son of man when He comes in His glory. The nations will be judged according to what they have done or not done to Israel, Jesus' brethren. What will happen to the nations afterwards though? We could sum it up by saying that they will taste the blessed outworkings of Jesus' work on the cross of Calvary. *"All nations* whom thou hast made shall come and worship before thee, O Lord; and shall glorify thy name" (Psalm 86:9). When we prayerfully consider the words of Zephaniah 3:8-10, we see three stages:

1. The judgment upon the nations through fire, "All the earth shall be devoured with the fire of my jealousy".

2. The nations will be cleansed through the judgment, "For then will I turn to the people a pure language" (v.9). This will mean the end of all cursing, blaspheming, backbiting and lying.

3. "That they may all call upon the name of the Lord, to serve him with one consent" (v.9b). This service for the Lord, which is only directed towards Jerusalem and Calvary, will be a glorious reality.

"From beyond the rivers of Ethiopia my suppliants, even the daughter of my dispersed, shall bring mine offering" (v.10). The great royal prophet Isaiah has the same testimony, "Woe is me! for I am undone; because I am a man of unclean lips, and I dwell in the midst of a people of unclean lips: for mine eyes have seen the King, the Lord of hosts" (Isaiah 6:5). The same is what will happen to the nations also. Before the judgment has been pronounced even, they are already judged, namely then when the Lord appears in great power and glory. Which is followed by the cleansing through judgment, "Then flew one of the seraphims unto me, having a live coal in his hand, which he had taken with the tongs from off the altar: and he *laid it upon my mouth, and said, Lo, this hath touched thy lips; and thine iniquity is taken away, and thy sin purged"* (Isaiah 6:6-7). Then Isaiah heard the voice of the Lord, *"Whom shall I send, and who will go for us? Then said I, Here am I; send me"* (Isaiah 6:8). True worship consists of total surrender to the Lord's service. If we, as children of God, have the right spiritual inner standing, the same stages are also present in our lives, on the grounds of the sacrifice at Calvary:

—We are judged, because we have seen the holiness of God in spirit.

Through His precious, shed blood, we are cleansed with a "live coal from off the altar" and judged through the judgment which was carried out on Him.

—On the grounds of these facts, we are able to serve Him with cleansed lips, which is the goal of all true worship of God.

This is exactly what will happen to the nations in the millennium. There are three reasons for the wonderful blessing on the nations:

1. Satan will be bound at that time so that his poisonous influences will be eliminated. Ephesians 6:12 will no longer apply to the nations because they will no longer have to fight with flesh and blood or with principalities, powers or rulers of the darkness. The source of evil, by which the nations were influenced and effected will have dried up so that the attacks of the enemy will be over.

2. The second cause of great blessing is far more

significant and glorious. Jesus Christ will then be Ruler and King and the whole world will come under His blessed influence and His peace will even extend to the animal world, *"The wolf and the lamb shall feed together, and the lion shall eat straw like the bullock: and dust shall be the serpents meat. They shall not hurt nor destroy in all my holy mountain, saith the Lord"* (Isaiah 65:25) In Habakkuk 2:14 we read that the whole world will be full of the glory of the Lord, *"For the earth shall be filled with the knowledge of the glory of the Lord, as the waters cover the sea"*. This immeasurable glory of the Lord which will fill the whole earth will also have wonderful consequences for mankind. Disease will be a rarity and people will live longer. When a person dies at the age of a hundred years old he will be counted a child, cf. Isaiah 65:20. The great pharmaceutical concerns which produce medicines and pills will soon have to change over to producing other products! A further consequence of the divine government is the complete absence of war. *"And he shall judge among the nations, and shall rebuke many people ... "* (Isaiah 2:4a). This means that there will be no more war because Jesus Christ will judge and settle all differences. From the same verse we see also that the entire weapon industry will have to change over to the production of peace products, *" ... and they shall beat their swords into plowshares, and their spears into pruninghooks"* (Isaiah 2:4b).

3. From this it is obvious that there will not be a military training center to be found in the world.

The last sentence of Isaiah 2:4 tells us this, *"Neither shall they learn war any more"*. The existing equipment and uniforms will even be destroyed, *"For every tramping warrior's war-boots and all his armour in the battle tumult and every garment rolled in blood shall be burned as fuel for the fire"* (Isaiah 9:5, Amplified Bible).

The cause of this blessing is Israel, for she will experience the fulfilment of the words of Romans 11:26-27, *"And so all Israel shall be saved: as it is written, There shall come out of Sion the Deliverer, and shall turn away ungodliness from Jacob: for this is my covenant unto them, when I shall take away their sins"*. Let us read again carefully Isaiah 2:2b-3a, *"And all nations shall flow unto it. And many people shall go and say, Come ye, and let us go up to the mountain of the Lord, to the house of the God of Jacob: and he will teach us of his ways, and we will walk in his paths"*. The judgment over Israel and her conversion will cause the nations to go to Jerusalem to learn of the ways of the Lord. Jerusalem will then become an international Bible School, free of all denominational spirits. This is the first result. The second result will be that through this gigantic Bible School, which will be open to all nations, a worldwide evangelistic movement will proceed from Israel, *"For out of Zion shall go forth the law, and the word of the Lord from Jerusalem"* (Isaiah 2:3b). In our case it is the other way around: first the people are evangelized and when they are won for the Lord they can go to Bible School. The conversion of the whole nation of Israel and the presence of the Lord Jesus Christ with His glorified

Church will have such a mighty impact that the Gentiles will be drawn to Jerusalem, as by a magnet, to come and learn there. This will initiate the evangelization. Here the question arises, Will it be necessary to evangelize in the millennium then? Yes! Satan will then be bound but sin will still be present in man.

In the millennium the relationship of the world to Jesus Christ will be quite different from what it is in our present times. While the true children of God are tolerated as strangers now, in the millennium the enemies of Jesus will be tolerated, but only if they submit themselves to His sovereign rule. It is obvious from many verses in the Bible that this submission is partly hypocrisy, for instance Psalm 18:43-45 and Psalm 66:3, *"Say to God, How awesome and fearfully glorious are Your works! Through the greatness of Your power shall your enemies submit themselves to You - with feigned and reluctant obedience"* (Amplified Bible). We must not forget that sin will be much more "sinful" in the millennium because the tempter will be absent. A person who is under the blessed influence of the Lord Jesus and yet resists the Lord is more guilty than ever before. The Scriptures also tell us that the sinner of a hundred years shall be accursed (Isaiah 65:20). Thus we see that in the millennium sin will still exist but grace will be infinitely greater. In the millennium the whole nation of Israel will be engaged in missionary work. It will no longer be the case that individuals on the mission field are reached through hard toil, for the Word of the Lord will be fulfilled, *"And the gospel of the kingdom shall be preached in all the*

*world for a witness unto all nations; and then
shall the end come"* (Matthew 24:14). Now we are
living in a missionary century but then it will be a
missionary millennium, in which God's promise to
Abraham will be literally fulfilled, *"And in thy
seed shall all the nations of the earth be blessed"*
(Genesis 22:18). Of this worldwide revival we are
told, *"Also the sons of the stranger, that join themselves to the Lord, to serve him, and to love the
name of the Lord, to be his servants, every one
that keepeth the sabbath from polluting it, and
taketh hold of my covenant; even them will I
bring to my holy mountain, and make them joyful
in my house of prayer: their burnt offerings and
their sacrifices shall be accepted upon mine altar:
for mine house shall be called an house of prayer
for all people"*(Isaiah 56:6-7). The temple in
Jerusalem will be the central point for all nations,
for there they will worship the Lord. The late Ben
Gurion said in 1950, "Jerusalem is not only the
capital of Israel and of world Judaism; according to
the words of the prophets, it will also be the
spiritual capital of the world". Since this statement
of Ben Gurion more than twenty years have
passed. We are coming nearer and nearer to the
fulfillment of these prophetic words. The first fruit
of the Israeli world evangelization will be a change
of heart within the nations. *"At that time they
shall call Jerusalem the throne of the Lord; and all
the nations shall be gathered unto it, to the name
of the Lord; to Jerusalem: neither shall they walk
any more after the imagination of their evil heart"*
(Jeremiah 3:17). Notice that we are not concerned
here with Christian missionary work amongst Jews
but the mission of Christ as going forth from the

"And the wolf also shall dwell with the lamb . . ."
(Isaiah 11:6).

Jews! Just how great the extent of this evangelistic movement amongst the nations will be is seen from the following text, *"For from the rising of the sun even unto the going down of the same my name shall be great among the Gentiles; and in every place incense shall be offered unto my name, and a pure offering: for my name shall be great among the heathen, saith the Lord of hosts"* (Malachi 1:11). Truly, Israel's conversion will be for the nations what the apostle Paul prophesied, *"For if the casting away of them be the reconciling of the world, what shall the receiving of*

them be, but life from the dead?" (Romans 11:15).
Israel, which for centuries was trodden down,
despised and mocked, will be the most glorious
nation of the world and will be made the head of
the nations (Deuteronomy 28:13).

If once the conversion of one single Israeli, Saul of
Tarsus, was enough to shake the Roman Empire,
how much greater will the effect be when Israel as
a nation turns to the Lord! Here conversion will take
place in the same way as Paul's, namely through
the appearance of Jesus Christ. Israel will exercise
the power of the King of all kings, the Lord Jesus
Christ, on earth. All the angels rejoice over one
sinner who repents, but the joy of the nations over
the presence of the Lord Jesus and His reign with
His Church, through Israel, will be indescribable.
We can imagine a little of this joy when we read
Psalm 96:10-13 for instance, *"Say among the
heathen that the Lord reigneth: the world also
shall be established that it shall not be moved: he
shall judge the people righteously. Let the heavens
rejoice, and let the earth be glad: let the sea roar,
and the fulness thereof. Let the field be joyful, and
all that is therein: then shall all the trees of the
wood rejoice before the Lord: for he cometh, for he
cometh to judge the earth: he shall judge the
world with righteousness, and the people with his
truth"*. This glorious statement of Scripture has
been Christianized for centuries but, together with
many other passages, it is a prophetic reference to
the millennium, the thousand-year reign of peace.
Let us remember that the creation has also sighed
for six thousand years under the rule of the prince
of this world, *"For ever the whole creation waits*

expectantly and longs earnestly for God's sons to be made known" (Romans 8:19, Amplified Bible).

To the question as to which nations will be gripped by this overpowering joy of salvation, the Word of the Lord also gives us the answer, namely, " . . . *the last shall be first"*. When we read in Zephaniah 3:10, *"From beyond the rivers of Ethiopia my suppliants, even the daughter of my dispersed, shall bring mine offering",* we think of the millions of people in Asia, Africa, S. America, etc., who have no knowledge of God, know nothing of Jesus Christ and do not know Israel either. From the following text we see that these too will be reached, *"And I will set a sign among them, and I will send those that escape of them unto the nations, to Tarshish, Pul, and Lud, that draw the bow, to Tubal and Javan, to the isles afar off, what have not heard my fame, neither have seen my glory; and they shall declare my glory among the Gentiles. And they shall bring all your brethren for an offering unto the Lord . . . "* (Isaiah 66:19-20a). In fact, even the beggars and tramps will be invited and also the undeveloped countries which, despite all the foreign aid they have received, still have heard nothing of God the Lord and His Son, Jesus Christ nor of Israel. These will obtain the promise, *"And in that day there shall be a root of Jesse,* (that is Jesus) *which shall stand for an ensign of the people; to it shall the Gentiles seek: and his rest shall be glorious"* (Isaiah 11:10).

This will have the following consequences for the political situation of the nations, *"In that day shall there be a highway out of Egypt to Assyria, and* the Assyrian shall come into Egypt, and the Egyptian into Assyria, and the Egyptians shall serve with the Assyrians. In that day shall Israel be the third with Egypt and with Assyria, even a blessing in the midst of the land: whom the Lord of hosts shall bless, saying, Blessed be Egypt my people, and Assyria the work of my hands, and Israel mine inheritance" (Isaiah 19: 23-25). This is a mysterious Word, for in view of the terrible hatred of the Egyptians and Syrians for Israel we can hardly imagine such an alliance. Let us recall what God promised Abraham, however, "In the same day the Lord made a covenant with Abram, saying, Unto thy seed have I given this land, from the river of Egypt unto the great river, the river Euphrates" (Genesis 15:18). Israel will no longer be the narrow strip of land between Jordan and the Mediterranean Sea. God will realize His promise in the millennium in a wonderful way. Israel is already clinging to this promise but the Arab countries and the rest of the world do not want to acknowledge it. Today we are witnessing the fulfillment of God's promise in Isaiah 19:1-3a, "The burden of Egypt. Behold, the Lord rideth upon a swift cloud, and shall come into Egypt: and the idols of Egypt shall be moved at his presence, and the heart of Egypt shall melt in the midst of it. And I will set the Egyptians against the Egyptians: and they shall fight every one against his brother, and every one against his neighbor; city against city, and kingdom against kingdom. And the spirit of Egypt shall fail in the midst thereof; and I will destroy the counsel thereof. Further we are told of the future of Egypt, "And the Egyptians will I give over into the hand *of a cruel lord; and a fierce king shall rule over them, saith the Lord, the Lord of hosts"* (Isaiah 19:4). Also that which we read in the following verses, 5 and 6, has begun to come about, *"And the waters shall fail from the sea, and the river shall be wasted and dried up. And they shall turn the rivers far away; and the brooks of defense shall be emptied and dried up: the reeds and flags shall wither".* According to newspaper reports, the huge Aswan dam project, built by the Russians, threatens to be a great failure in Egypt's history. The water of the Nile, which is responsible for the fertility of the land, is now being diverted, but not only that! Egypt will be converted under the mighty blows of the Antichrist, *"And the Lord shall smite Egypt: he shall smite and heal it: and they shall return even to the Lord, and he shall be intreated of them, and shall heal them"* (Isaiah 19:22). Possibly Egypt will then produce many of the lost ten tribes of Israel, *"In that day shall five cities in the land of Egypt speak the language of Canaan, and swear to the Lord of hosts; one shall be called, The city of destruction"* (Isaiah 19:22). The Amplified Bible translates the latter "the City of the Sun or Destruction". Do we not see a light from above beginning to shine upon the hidden ten tribes? In another verse the prophet Isaiah says of this alliance of nations, *"And it shall come to pass in that day, that the Lord shall set his hand again the second time to recover the remnant of his people, which shall be left, from Assyria, and from Egypt . . . "* (Isaiah 11:11). The significance of this threefold union for the rest of the world is seen from chapter 19 of Isaiah, *"In that day shall Israel be the third with Egypt and with Assyria, even a blessing in the midst of the land: whom the Lord of hosts shall bless, saying, Blessed be Egypt my people, and Assyria the work of my hands, and Israel mine inheritance"* (Isaiah 19: 24-25). Six things which characterize the events concerning the nations are also decisive for the believers in our time.

1. JUDGMENT. God will judge the nations righteously. Children of God go through the judgment of Calvary. They are crucified with Christ and will be glorified with Him.

2. CLEANSING. Isaiah was cleansed with a fiery coal from the altar. In this way the nations will also be cleansed and have pure lips. Children of God are cleansed in the precious blood of Jesus which He shed when He was judged in our stead.

3. HUNGER FOR THE WORD OF GOD. All the Gentiles will come to Jerusalem and say, Come and let us learn the ways of the Lord! Whoever has experienced a profound cleansing in the blood of Jesus also has hunger for the Word of God.

4. WORSHIP AND DEVOTION. The nations will worship the Lord in Jerusalem. Nobody who has experienced the glory of the Lamb in his life lacks the spirit of worship.

5. THE UNION OF ISRAEL WITH HER BROTHERS. The Syrians and Egyptians are relatives of Israel and from these lands part of the ten "lost" tribes will come. We are one as brothers and sisters in the Lord. According to the measure in which we

are judged, cleansed and hungry for God's Word shall we have the spirit of worship (1 John 1:7).

6. ISRAEL WILL BE A BLESSING ON EARTH, together with her brothers. This is also the case for you and me. You are only a blessing to your surroundings, your city, your country, for the world, according to the measure of your fellowship with Jesus.

To summarize let us consider again the three groups of people who will have part in the millennium:
— THE CHURCH OF JESUS CHRIST. She is the Holy of holies, in heaven. She has part in the royal sovereignty of Jesus Christ. We shall be kings and priests.
— ISRAEL. She is God's sanctuary on earth. She is God's instrument of jurisdiction and proclaimer of salvation.
— THE NATIONS. These will be in the forecourt and will worship God the Lord as did once the twelve tribes of Israel.

Let us repeat once more what the consequence is for us who should be in the Holy of holies in the millennium. It is decisively important that we live in the Holy of Holies now! This is the will of God and He invites us to do so. *"Having therefore, brethren, boldness to enter into the holiest by the blood of Jesus . . . Let us draw near with a true heart"* (Hebrews 10:19 and 22a).

CHAPTER 8

WHAT WILL HAPPEN AFTER THE MILLENNIUM?

"And when the thousand years are expired, Satan shall be loosed out of his prison, and shall go out to deceive the nations which are in the four quarters of the earth, Gog and Magog, to gather them together to battle: the number of whom is as the sand of the sea. And they went up on the breadth of the earth, and compassed the camp of the saints about, and the beloved city; and fire came down from God out the heaven, and devoured them" (Revelation 20:7-9).

Here we have come to a most serious time period; it is the end of the sabbath or millennium. The big question arises: Why is the thousand year reign of peace only temporary? My answer is; it is not temporary but eternal. Even though the kingdom of God on this earth will only last for a thousand years it will nevertheless continue into eternity through an interlude. In the Bible, numbers ususally refer to space and time. We read in revelation 20:7a *"And when the thousand years were expired. . ."* When this thousand years are over "God's demonstration" showing the world what God means by righteous and peace will also have come to an end-in all aspects of life i.e. politics and economics etc. What a glorious period of time that will be when God Himself is united with this earthly kingdom and Jesus Christ reigns as King. The millenium will start after the completion of our present time of grace. God the Lord does everything in His own perfect time and He has given man six thousand years to bring the earth under the law—and two thousand years under grace. The period "without the law" could be described as follows: Do not do it and you will live, or, do not sin so that you will not die. Of the period "under the law" we could say: Do it and you will live, or, keep God's commandments. But then God changed it around by the giving of His Son Jesus, so that we can say of the era "under grace": Live and you will then be able to do it-through Calvary. This is a gift of the living God. God's intention for our present age of grace is clearly described in Acts 15:14, *". . .how God at the first did visit the Gentiles, to take out of them a people for his name."* For the period after this God says, *"After this I will return, and will build again the tabernacle of David, which is fallen down; and I will build again the ruins thereof, and I will set it up"* (Acts 15:16). What will be His reason for doing this? *"That the residue of men might seek after the Lord, and all the Gentiles, upon whom my name is called, saith the Lord, who doeth all these things"* (Acts 15:17). We must never think that God does anything indefinite, for, *"Known unto God are all his works from the beginning of the world."* (Acts 15:18). He has numbered all the stars and calls them by their name. He has also counted your days and years until they are complete; He counts your tears until there are enough.

The millennium will be a specific and limited period of time in the history of salvation of the world. In our time Satan is not yet bound but is very active in his tremendous compulsion to destroy. During the thousand years, however, he and his servants will be prevented from coming into the world to deceive mankind. He will then be bound and kept in the bottomless pit (Revelation 20:2-3, *"And he laid hold on the dragon, that old serpent, which is the Devil, and Satan, and bound him a thousand years, and cast him into the bottomless pit, and shut him up, and set a seal upon him, that he should deceive the nations no more, till the thousand years should be fulfilled: and after that he must be loosed a little season."*

All we can do now is to plead with people on behalf of Christ to be reconciled with God and serve the Lord in fear and rejoice with trembling (Psalm 2:3). Later men will have no choice but will have to obey the commands which are given them, for Jesus will then be exercising His power. During the millennium the nations will have only one alternative: to obey the immortal Priest King. For a thousand years God Himself, through Jesus Christ, will manifest the difference between the government of His Son and the dictatorship of Satan. In Jesus we have eternal life but under Satan, death and destruction. We can experience this already now in our own lives. The government of Jesus in the indiviual is a blessed one. He Himself says, *"My yoke is easy, and my burden is light."* In contrast, the government of Satan is cruel.

The blessed kingdom of peace of the Lord will have an apparently sudden end,*"And when the thousands years are expired, Satan shall be loosed out of his prison, and shall go out to deceive the nations which are in the four quarters of the earth, Gog and Magog, to gather them together to battle: the number of whom is as the sand of the sea...* (Revelation 20:7-8). Why must this happen? Over this event lies a divine "must" of God. Satan will be set free again after his thousand year imprisonment so it will be obvious that he has not changed and that his term of punishment was in vain. Further, it will also prove that the majority of people, despite all the wonderful outward blessing which they received during the thousand years, did not let themselves be inwardly renewed. At the end of the millennium it will be apparent that Satan has remained the same and that man as such has not changed, despite the thousand year imprisonment of Satan and the paradise conditions for man. Here we can only wonder at the patience of God in punishment as well as in blessing. Through the prophets, however, we hear His lamentations, *"Why should ye be stricken any more? ye will revolt more and more: the whole head is sick, and the whole heart faint".*(Isaiah 1:5), or, *I have set thee for a tower and a fortress among my people, that thou mayest know and try their way. They are all grievous revolters, walking with slanders: They are brass and iron; they are all corrupters. The bellows are burned, the lead is consumed of the fire; the founder melteth in vain: for the wicked are not plucked away* (Jeremiah 6:27-29). This is millennium, but already in our days we come to the same frightful conclusion-

neither by God's goodness nor by His judgments do people come to repentance. Following the millennium when Satan is free again he will pursue Gog and Magog (this is a collective name for the nations) and they will be receptive to the satanic spirit of rebellion, *"And shall go out to deceive the nations which are in the four quarters of the earth, Gog and Magog, to gather them together to battle: the number of whom is as the sand of the sea. And they went up on the breadth of the earth, and compassed the camp of the saints about, and the beloved city.* (Revelation 20:8-9). It is not the same as before the millennium when Satan sent out his servants to deceive the kings of the earth. In the millennium there is no other king besides the ONE: Jesus Christ.

Strangely enough Satan will go to the four ends of the earth, turning his attention to those nations which live furthest away and in the most unknown parts of the earth. He has to go so far away because there is nothing more he can do in the beloved city with its holy people who are united with Jesus Christ their King. Here is an apparent parallel in Satan's behaviour; just as he made his first attempt at deception in paradise on a woman, the weaker and more gullible vessel, so he will use the same method in his last attempt when he goes to distant heathen lands which were only slightly touched by the knowledge of God during the millennium. These will be receptive to Satan's suggestions and become willing instruments in his hand. Here we can learn an important lesson for our personal lives: the less we know God and the Lamb the more we are open to satanic temptations and to the spirit of rebellion against God and the Lamb. Woe to those who through prayerlessness do not live within sanctuary, for the enemy is very active even in our times. He goes around and knocks at your door also, trying to move you to rebellion by means of his soft talk. Therefore let us watch and pray.

How is it possible that the enemy can actually cause men who have experienced the wonderful government of Jesus Christ for a thousand years to become enemies of God? I think there is only one reason; when the old nature remains in a person he moves away from the Holy City, which means that although he is touched outwardly by the blessings of the Lamb, because he does not follow the lamb, he remains inwardly the same as he was. This also applies to us. That is why the post-millenial events are a serious warning for us all. The end result of this final divine judgment proves the necessity of it. Through it the extent of the nation's hypocrisy will be revealed-otherwise they would continue in hypocrisy. Satanic temptation will bring to light those who have rebellious hearts which have been covered by religious camouflage. Here again we see another parallel: Satan is using the same methods today as he will do after the millennium. The end of the millennium is nothing other than the beginning of the eternal kingdom.

We, as the Church of Jesus Christ, are therefore standing on the border between time and eternity. The beginning of our eternal existence is actually now in this age.

When we consider the terrible end of the rebellious nations it is most striking how quickly and thoroughly the adversary is dealt with; it is described in twelve words, . . .*and fire came down from God out of heaven, and devoured them"* (Revelation 20:9b). Here we have the final collision between the Holiest and the unholiest. Although the camp of the saints is surrounded, the immortal saints take not the slightest notice of the enemy because in their midst is the King of all kings and His Word says, *"He that toucheth you toucheth the apple of His eye"* (Zechariah 2:8b). Therefore desite the proximity of the enemy they do not need to fear, nor do they need to fight, for *"The Lord shall fight for you, and ye shall hold your peace"* (Exodus 14:14).

The children of Korah, in the Old Testament, already saw the end of the millennium and prophesied about this assurance. *"God is our refuge and strength, a very present help in trouble. Therefore will not we fear, though the earth be removed, and though the mountains be carried into the midst of the sea; though the waters thereof roar and be troubled, though the mountains shake with the swelling thereof. There is a river, the streams whereof shall make glad the city of God, the holy place of the tabernacles of the most HIGH. God is in the midst of her; she shall not be moved: God shall help her, and that right early. The heathen raged, the kingdoms were moved: he uttered his voice, the earth melted. The Lord of hosts is with us; the God of Jacob is our refuge"* (Psalm 46:1-7). *"IS IN THE MIDST OF HER. . ."* For this reason, never allow yourself to be robbed of your strengths and energy, for your "camp" is untouchable if you are in Jesus! *"The name of the Lord is a strong tower: the righteous runneth into it, and is safe"* (Proverbs 18:10).

According to Revelation 20:10 the Satanic trinity will meet a frightful end, *"And the devil that deceived them was cast into the lake of fire and brimstone, where the beast and the false prophet are, and shall be tormented day and night for ever and ever."* With this we come to the beginning of the final judgment before the great white throne. Together with John, we too can see in spirit this last settlement. *"And I saw a great white throne, and him that sat on it.."* (Revelation 20:11a). It is important that we distinguish between the three different judgment thrones, because before the so-called "last judgment" there are two other thrones of judgment. The first throne is for the CHURCH OF JESUS CHRIST; after the rapture all of us without exception will have to appear before Jesus, *"For we must all appear before the judgment seat of Christ; that everyone may receive the things done in his body* (his pay- Amplified Bible), *according to that he hath done, whether it be good or bad"* (2 Corinthians 5:10). The seriousness of this judgment is seen in the next verse, *"Knowing therefore the terror of the Lord, we persuade men"* (v.11). This judgment will not deal with the question of who is lost and who is saved,-for all true members of the Church are saved-but with the question of REWARDS due, or not due, to children of God.

Seven years after this the second throne will be erected on earth. This is called the "THRONE OF HIS GLORY" in Matthew 25:31b. The Church does not need to appear before this throne. Here, each NATION will be asked what it has done with Israel, with the brethren of the Lord. This too will be either judged or rewarded accordingly by the Lord.

The third throne, which we have already mentioned-the "GREAT WHITE THRONE"-will be erected on earth at the end of the millennium at the end of seven thousand years of human history. The second resurrection will take place at this time and judgment will be passed on all those who have not already been judged. *"And I saw the dead, small and great, stand before God; and the books were opened: and another book was opened, which is the book of life: and the dead were judged out of those things which were written in the books, according to their works. And the sea gave up the dead which were in it; and death and hell delivered up the dead which were in them: and they were judged every man according to their words"* (Revelation 20:12-13). This is the very last thing God does before He creates the new heaven and the new earth. These dead ones, small and great, will now stand not only before a great throne but before a "GREAT WHITE THRONE"; every dark dead will be brought to the light in His all-penetrating brightness. All who had no part in the first resurrection will now stand before the face of Him who sits on the throne. The most terrible thing is that there will no longer be any possiblity of escaping. As it is written in Revelation 20:11b,

"...from whose face the earth and the heaven fled away; and there was found no place for them." Those who ignored and rejected Jesus and the salvation He offered are confronted by His exalted Majesty. May the Lord grant that you are not present at that time, but are rather with those of whom it is written, *"Blessed and holy is he that hath part in the first resurrection: on such the second death hath no power, but they shall be priests of God and of Christ, and shall reign with him a thousand years"* (Revelation 20:6).

This creates another important question: What will happen to the millions of people who are called to the second and last resurrection? Judgment is passed on them in silence; there will be no more talking, only an opening of the books, and of the book of life. What is written-or rather what is found lacking in the book of life-will condemn them. These will then suffer the second death, *"And death and hell were cast into the lake of fire. This is the second death"* (Revelation 20:14). Perhaps you would like to ask: What is this second death? This is the death which does not kill but separates one eternally from God. That is the hell which Jesus suffered for us when He cried out, *"My God, my God, why hast thou forsaken me?"* Hell is the place where God turns away from. In this silent act of judgment, where the exalted majesty of God lets the books speak, the blood of Jesus Christ is lacking. There is no time left to repent, it is too late, because of the imminence of the new heaven and the new earth. *"And I saw a new heaven and a new earth: for the first heaven and the first earth were passed away; and there was no more sea"* (Revelation 21:1). The first things are passed away! "Oh", many will now say, "how glad I am that I shall take part in the first resurrection and not need to appear before the great white throne! "That is true, if you really are a child of God; you will appear before the judgment seat of Christ. But many forget one thing: even today we already have to do with this same God whose eyes see everything and from whom nothing can be hidden, *"..but all things are naked and opened unto the eyes of him with whom we have to do"* (Hebrews4:13b). This same letter to the Hebrews says, *"It is a fearful thing to fall into the hands of the living God"* (chapter 10:31). Do you wonder what this really means? Satan does not want you to be able to stand before the judgment seat of Christ. ON THE CONTRARY, HE WANTS TO BLUR YOUR VISION FOR THE SERIOUSNESS OF THESE FACTS SO THAT YOU WILL BE PUT TO SHAME ON THAT DAY WHEN YOU STAND BEFORE Jesus Christ. If you now present yourself in spirit before the throne of God what is the reflection you see? What comes to light when you stand before His face now? Are you willing just now to allow God to reveal all the hidden things in you? The thoughts of your heart, your secret grudge, your hidden uncleanness, your worldliness and your joking spirit? It is a matter of utmost urgency that you set yourself to be cleansed by the blood of Jesus so that you will not be ashamed before Him at His coming. It is written, *"And every man that hath this hope in him purifieth himself, even as he is pure"* (1 John 3:3). Inspired by the Holy Spirit, Peter wrote the following for our serious consideration, *"Seeing then that all these things shall be dissolved, what manner of persons ought ye be in all holy conversation and godliness, Looking for and hasting unto the coming of the day of God, wherein the heavens being of fire shall be dissolved, and the elements shall melt with fervent heat? Nevertheless we, according to his promise, look for new heavens and a new earth, wherein dwelleth righteousness."*

(2Peter 3:11)

O earth, earth, earth, hear the word of the LORD!

By the Same Author

ISRAEL'S GOD DOES NOT LIE

by Wim Malgo **$2.95**

This book is a must for every serious Christian, who is waiting for the Second Coming of Christ. The Author penetrates deeply into the Spiritual background of the latest events in the Middle East, including the "Yom Kippur War". Illuminating these events in the light of Bible Prophecy, many astonishing truths are clearly revealed as never before. As the spiritual tribulation for Christians will suddenly end in the bliss of the Rapture . . . so will Israel's physical tribulation climax into the revelation of their Messiah, Jesus Christ. Some of the Chapters contained in this book, • The Yom Kippur War • Jerusalem's Border • Will the Antichrist come from the tribe of Dan? • The Destruction of the Nations • The First and the Last King of Jerusalem . . . and more.

1 book $2.95 **2 books $5.00** **5 books $10.00**

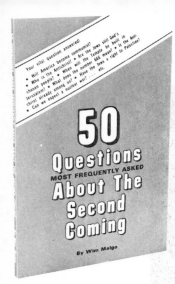
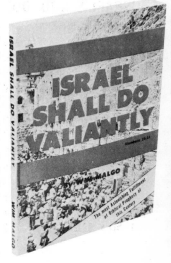

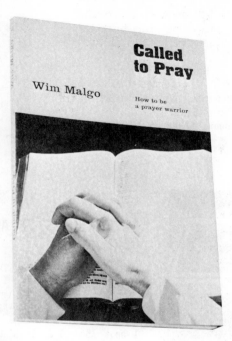

CALLED TO PRAY
by Wim Malgo
$2.45

An enlightening and reliable guidance to victorious prayerlife. Read in this book how Prophets, Apostles, Priests and Kings used PRAYER to overcome the enemy. Tells how your life in Christ can become a powerful testimony. PRAYER is one of the most important subjects in your Bible.

17 INSPIRING CHAPTERS TO FILL YOUR HEART A REAL TREASURE IN EVERY CHRISTIAN HOME

1 book $2.45   3 books $6.00   5 books $8.00

THE RAPTURE

by Wim Malgo 75c

This booklet has a well prepared, scripturally grounded message about the great event expected to take place any time . . . the RAPTURE of the Church!

Gives light on . . . How will it happen? . . . who will take part? . . . what must I do? . . . and many other important questions answered.

VALUABLE FOR BIBLE STUDY

1 book 75c 3 books $2.00 5 books $3.00

SEVEN SIGNS OF A BORN AGAIN PERSON

by Wim Malgo 75c

A crystal clear outline how to recognize a truly born-again person.

Answers vital questions every one should know.

SEVEN BIBLICAL SIGNS

1 book 75c 3 books $2.00 5 books $3.00

THE GREAT MYSTERY OF THE RAPTURE

by Wim Malgo 55c

This book will lead you through the Bible and reveal many deep secrets about this great event . . . Why the Bible speaks about it as a mystery . . . How come the dead in Christ will rise FIRST? . . . Are there any signs for the rapture? Why will the Lord meet us in the AIR? . . . and many more soul stirring questions clearly revealed!

1 book 55c 5 books $2.00 12 books $4.00

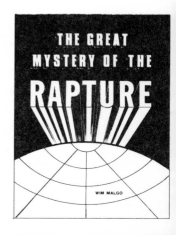

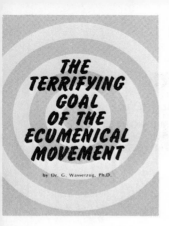

THE TERRIFYING GOAL OF THE ECUMENICAL MOVEMENT

by Dr. G. Wasserzug, Ph.D.   95c

Facts, figures and opinion are carefully analyzed and compared with the unfailing truth of the Holy Scriptures.

This book unvails the basic errors of the most fateful and dangerous organization in the history of the Church.

INDISPENSABLE FOR EVERY CHRISTIAN
1 book 95c   4 books $3.00   8 books $5.00

THE BIBLE IS TRUE!

by Dr. G. Wasserzug Ph.D.   75c

Bible critics and modern Theologians are silenced when confronted with this book. A compact outline about how the Bible proves that THE BIBLE IS TRUE.

1 book 75c   3 books $2.00   5 books $3.00

To order use last Page

ORDER FORM

Fill in, Clip, and Mail this Whole Page to:

MIDNIGHT CALL   **In Canada: THE MIDNIGHT CALL**
P.O. BOX 704   **P.O. BOX 3531, STA. B**
HAMILTON, OH. 45012   **CALGARY, ALBERTA T2M 4M2**

☐ Please send me the following books I have checked below:

Qty.	Title	Price	Total
___	20th Century Handwriting on the Wall	$3.95	___
___	50 Questions About The Second Coming	1.95	___
___	Israel Shall Do Valiantly	2.65	___
___	Israel's God Does Not Lie	2.95	___
___	Called To Pray	2.45	___
___	Seven Signs Of A Born-Again Person	.75	___
___	The Rapture	.75	___
___	The Bible Is True	.75	___
___	1,000 Years Peace	1.95	___
___	The Terrifying Goal of The Ecumenical Movement	.95	___
___	Jerusalem, Focal Point of the World	2.25	___
___	The Last Days	2.45	___
___	On The Border of Two Worlds	.95	___
___	Group Dynamics New Tool of the Antichrist	.95	___
___	Signs and Wonders	.95	___

☐ Enclosed $2.00, please send a one-year
   subscription to MIDNIGHT CALL magazine.

Total Enclosed $ _____

NAME   Mr.
        Mrs. _____
        Miss   Please Print

STREET _____

CITY _____ STATE _____ ZIP _____